# BARNES & NOBLE BASICS

# your job
# interview

by Cynthia Ingols and Mary Shapiro

BARNES
& NOBLE
BOOKS
NEW YORK

Other titles in the **Barnes & Noble Basics**™ series:
**Barnes & Noble Basics** *Using Your PC*
**Barnes & Noble Basics** *Wine*
**Barnes & Noble Basics** *In the Kitchen*
**Barnes & Noble Basics** *Getting in Shape*
**Barnes & Noble Basics** *Saving Money*
**Barnes & Noble Basics** *Getting a Job*
**Barnes & Noble Basics** *Using the Internet*
**Barnes & Noble Basics** *Retiring*
**Barnes & Noble Basics** *Using Your Digital Camera*
**Barnes & Noble Basics** *Getting Married*
**Barnes & Noble Basics** *Grilling*
**Barnes & Noble Basics** *Giving a Presentation*
**Barnes & Noble Basics** *Buying a House*
**Barnes & Noble Basics** *Volunteering*
**Barnes & Noble Basics** *Getting a Grant*
**Barnes & Noble Basics** *Getting into College*
**Barnes & Noble Basics** *Golf*
**Barnes & Noble Basics** *Résumés and Cover Letters*

# introduction

"I have wonderful news," my friend Paul exclaimed. "I have a job interview next week! I really want the job, but interviewing is so nerve-racking. What if they ask me why I left my last job? Should I tell them I disagreed with my boss? And I never did finish my bachelor's degree. Should I mention that? I'm not sure what to say and what to leave out. What should I do?"

If this sounds like you, relax! The answers to all your interview dilemmas are right here in **Barnes & Noble Basics** *Your Job Interview*. We'll walk you through everything you need to know about interviewing with confidence so you can land that job. We cover the entire process, from getting that first phone call to negotiating an offer. You'll learn how to highlight your past job successes and handle sticky situations like a career change or a murky job history. Plus, we'll show you how to put your best face forward when it comes to grooming and manners. You'll learn savvy responses to common (and not so common) curveball questions, and you'll get expert advice on interviewing with recruiters, future colleagues, and the "big boss."

Knowing how to present yourself in an interview is not just the key to your next job, it's a skill that will serve you well throughout your entire career. All the tools you need to master the art of interviewing are right here at your fingertips. Let's get started!

Barb Chintz
Editorial Director, the **Barnes & Noble Basics**™ series

# table of contents

## Chapter 1

# the screening interview

# the hiring process

## Prepare for each phase of it

Your résumé is done—phew! And you are about to start sending it out to several job ads you have spied in the newspaper or in your company's listing of internal job openings. You are good to go. If all goes well, your résumé will spark a hiring process that will end with you in a new job.

There are several phases to this hiring process. While your résumé is out doing its work, it's a good idea to start preparing for the next few phases you will encounter. The first phase is the phone call. This call can simply be a means of setting up a time for you to come in and be interviewed. Or that first phone call can be a **phone interview**—a 30- to 60-minute interview that is used to screen candidates. Getting interviewed over the phone is a good sign. It means you have made the very first cut! These days more and more job candidates are being screened over the phone before they even get their foot in the door. For this reason, you should be prepared to state your case over the phone (more on that in the next few pages). The good news is that the preparation you do for a phone screening will apply to an in-person interview as well.

The second phase is the **in-person interview**. This meeting can be with the actual person you will be working for or it can be a screening interview conducted by a human resource manager or a person from the department you hope to be working in. Here you will be asked key questions (see pages 48–49) and perhaps be required to take a few tests (see pages 36–37).

Depending on the type and level of job you are after and the size of the company, you may have to come back for more interviews. So be prepared for the third phase: **call-back interviews**. Here you may meet with various members of the team you may be working with or other department heads who need to sign off on your hiring. These stages require a good deal of patience on your part, so be prepared.

## ASK THE EXPERTS

### I got a call to set up a time for an interview. My days are wide open. When is the best time for interviews?

If possible, schedule your interview between 9 and 11 A.M. People are more alert and interviews are more productive in the morning. Try to avoid having an interview in the late afternoon when everyone's energy level is down.

### How long does it take to actually get a job?

That all depends. If you have contacts and there is an opening you can fill to perfection, one interview may result in a job offer the same day. Sounds nice, but remember that an easy hire can be an easy fire. The rule of thumb is that for every $10,000 of salary you want, add a month to your job search. In other words, if you want a job paying $60,000, expect your search to take six months. That kind of job search involves research, networking, revising your résumé, and, of course, interviewing.

## Good Phone Etiquette

Create a positive first impression, even if it's just a five-minute phone call to set up an interview time. Pay attention to how the caller identifies herself. Try to connect with her by using her name, but don't be too casual. It's better to be too formal and address her as "Ms." than to offend her by using her first name. And avoid casual greetings such as, "Hey, what's happening?" You want to convey that you're professional and capable over the phone. Do not be curt or unduly friendly. Do not bring up issues the caller can't cover—for example, questions about salary or benefits. Before you hang up, verify the interview time, date, and location. Get the name, job title, and phone number of the contact person in case you need to reschedule. You could also restate your interest in the job. Then thank her for inviting you to come in.

If employers will be calling you at home, make sure the message on your answering machine or voice mail is professional. Save the jokes and silly background music for after you've been hired.

# getting organized

## Keep a paper trail of your job search

Before you start sending out those résumés, you should decide on the system you're going to use for organizing your contacts, phone calls, and interviews. Everyone has a system that works for him or her, so the best idea is to stick with what you know rather than adopting some complex new system that's just going to trip you up.

You may decide to keep your notes in a job notebook, organize them on your computer, or both. Either way you do it, you need to be consistent about keeping it up-to-date; otherwise you can easily lose track of important details or job tips.

Your notebook is where you will gather every piece of information related to your job search, starting with the ads you reply to and the résumés and cover letters you send out. Keep a page for each ad or cover letter. Make note of when the letter was sent, whether you received a call about it, and how you followed up.

When you land an interview, write down the time, date, location, and other important information, such as the name of the person you'll be meeting and his title. You may also want to use your notebook to brainstorm about the questions you want to ask.

After each interview, write down key details, including impressions of the company and the interviewer, topics covered, any potential concerns, and the next steps you need to take. When you get to the final interview rounds, it's also a good idea to write down any tentative offers or agreements made, in case any discrepancies emerge later on when the offer is being finalized.

In your notebook, you should also keep a record of what you do each day to further your job search, including contacts you make, informal conversations you have, job fairs you attend, recruiters you call, or anything you read online or in the newspaper about jobs.

With your failproof system in place, you're ready to go!

_AD_  _Job_: Public Service Fellowship at City Year, Inc.

        Date Posted:    January 24, 2003
        Posted:         Monster.com
        Salary:         not included in ad
        Contact:        Caryn Pan, Senior VP Human Potential
                        City Year, Inc.
                        230 Washington Street, Boston, MA

_SENT_: Résumé and cover letter, January 26, 2003

_CALLED THEM_: February 4
                Talked to Michele in HR (617-333-2123)
                Told that they would contact candidates mid-February

_CALLED THEM_: February 20
                Talked to Michele
                Told they are awaiting final grant and then they'll call
                NOTE: Call back March 1

_THEY CALLED_: February 27
                Interview set up March 11, 8:30 A.M.
                With: Tom Darry, Director of HR
                NOTE: Check Web site for directions, mission of org.

_INTERVIEW_: March 11
                Met with Tom Darry
        Things he liked about me: social work undergrad and MBA, long
                experience with community service, volunteering, experience
                in Outward Bound, finance skills
        Challenges he faces: constant pressure on budget, doing more
                with less, turnover of skilled staff, managing volunteers
        Next step: They'll call in 2 weeks if meeting with Caryn Pan

_FOLLOW UP_: March 12
                Sent thank you (copy attached)

# the phone interview

**Prepare stellar responses now instead of having to think on your feet**

**W**hat can you expect from a phone interview? Fortunately, the questions you get over the phone are pretty much the same ones you eventually get in an in-person interview. Preparing for the standard questions now before the phone rings will give you a leg up should you get a phone interview. Having some solid responses under your belt can give you the confidence you need to handle any surprises. Here are some of the questions you'll most likely be asked.

## "Tell me about yourself."

While you may groan when you hear this one, it's actually a great opportunity for you. Use it to advertise your best attributes. Your answer should be kept to less than two minutes and include:

- a brief description of your relevant work background and education
- a sentence about three or four of your main strengths
- a story or two to illustrate those strengths
- a statement outlining your career plans, how you'd like to use and develop your skills, and how you can contribute to this organization

Consider your answer your positioning statement. In fact, this question is so advantageous that if the interviewer doesn't start out with it, try to squeeze it in by saying, "Before I answer that question, it may be helpful if I first give you background about myself."

## "Why would you like to work here?"

Share some specific information you've learned about the company. This shows that you take initiative, come prepared, and are able to make criteria-based decisions (all attributes valued by a potential employer).

**Example:** "I was impressed that *Money* magazine named you one of the best companies for women. The article stated that your high retention rate for senior female executives was due to the challenging assignments and candid performance feedback they are given. I want to work for a company that is going to stretch me in that way."

## "What are your weaknesses?"

How you talk about your weaknesses is more important than which ones you bring up. Some strategies:

■ State that you know of no weaknesses that would impact your ability to perform in this job. You could add an example of a weakness that wouldn't be relevant in this situation, like not being good at programming your VCR.

■ State a past weakness and describe how you've overcome it. "I used to have a problem with procrastination. A colleague helped me by suggesting that I get through two small tasks each morning by 10 A.M. It gave me a great feeling of accomplishment that paved the way for tackling larger projects. This system works really well for me."

■ State a weakness as too much of a good thing. "I'm always demanding more of myself than I can probably ever accomplish."

■ State a weakness as a preference. "I really enjoy getting into the details of a job and identifying all the specifics of a project, but I know I also need to keep the big picture in mind!"

## FIRST PERSON SUCCESS STORY

### First Impressions Count

The call was just to set up an interview, but I decided to start my interview then and there. I asked for the caller's name. It was Betty and she was very nice. I told her how enthusiastic I was about the job and asked her who the interview was with and how long it might be. She gave me a quick run-down on how interviews are handled. Turns out she was my future boss's assistant and my enthusiasm impressed her so much, she mentioned it to her boss. I'm sure it helped me land the job.

—Emily S., New Orleans, Louisiana

# smart phone tips

## Make your phone interview stand out

How do you impress a screener? There are a number of ways. For starters, it's always a good idea to show your knowledge of the company you want to work for. As one human resources manager of a large bank says: "I'm listening to hear if you have done your homework. Are you prepared for our conversation? Do you understand how we're different from the bank down the street?"

Next, show that you have good communication skills. Explain concisely your understanding of what the job is and your qualifications for it. Respond smartly to such questions as "Why are you interested in this position?"

Be ready to discuss salary requirements. If asked what salary you expect, you might answer, "I would expect market rates for this position to be . . ." or "I think my range could be $X to $X, based on the industry standard." Try to find out more about the position before pinning yourself down to a number, and be flexible.

When the phone interview is coming to a close, ask how you should follow up on your conversation. Then do so. If e-mail is the appropriate approach, send a short, thoughtful e-mail advancing your candidacy. One recruiter reports that of the approximate 1,000 telephone interviews she has conducted, she has received only two or three thank-you e-mails.

### No-Nos

**The interviewer asks you one question and you answer another.** Listen carefully. If you do not understand the question, ask for clarification. However, don't dodge questions that make you uncomfortable. You'll only sink your ship.

**You go on and on, and on and on, and on and on some more.** In other words, you conduct a monologue. One recruiter says that she stops listening and starts answering e-mail whenever a candidate drones on with no awareness of how he or she is coming across.

**You ask about salary and benefits.** Wrong. Wait until the interviewer asks what your salary expectations are. That's a signal that the company is interested in you.

## What Do Screeners Do?

Screeners are people who collect résumés and responses to job ads and select applicants to be interviewed. They may also conduct first-round interviews by phone or in person, then pass along their candidate choices to the hiring manager. They may work in the HR department of a company or they may be outside recruiters working with a company on a contract basis to fill a position.

# How Screeners Work

The person calling you has one task at hand: to eliminate unqualified candidates. This is because the company doesn't have the time to interview in person everyone who looks good on paper. Here's how the screening process usually works:

■ The hiring manager talks with a human resources (HR) manager about the job opening in question and the strengths and weaknesses of the last person who filled it. They discuss whether or not the requirements of the job have changed. Ideally, the HR manager comes away with a good sense of the skills, talents, and personal requirements for the position.

■ After advertising the job, the HR department might receive hundreds of résumés. An HR person is assigned the task of reviewing the résumés. For résumés sent by e-mail, he or she may use software that searches for keywords matching the job description. The resumes that make the cut (anywhere from 5 to 20) are then sent to the hiring manager.

■ The hiring manager lets HR know which candidates should go through a first-round phone interview. Typically this is six to eight candidates, but it can be as few as three or four.

■ The HR manager assigns a screener to conduct a telephone interview with each candidate for 30 minutes to 1 hour. (For more on this see page 175.) The screener sends a "go" or "no go" recommendation to the hiring manager.

■ The list is winnowed down. Those making the cut then get a call asking them to come for an interview. The interview will most likely involve meeting both the HR manager and the hiring manager.

# crafting success stories

## How to bring your accomplishments to life

You usually have 30 to 60 minutes to convince the phone interviewer that you are the person for the job. So what do you say? Think through your work history and look for things that show off your talents, skills, or personality traits. Did you redesign an office procedure that resulted in greater reporting accuracy? Did you get two departments to work together after a long-standing conflict? These success stories will be what distinguishes you from the rest of the pack. In preparing for your interview, you need to craft five or six of them, each two minutes long, describing key professional, task-oriented, or work-oriented achievements. To make it easy, use the START format.

**S** What was the Situation? Where and when did your action take place?

**T** What was the Trouble? What obstacles, challenges, or problems called for your action?

**A** What Action did you take?

**R** What were the Results or outcomes? Can you quantify those results—how many, how large, what percent?

**T** What are the Transferable skills you used that you can bring to this job?

It may take several hours to write these stories, but it will be well worth it. You can use them in the body of your cover letter to solicit jobs as well as during your in-person interviews to bring your skills and abilities to life.

These stories enable an interviewer to quickly identify what kind of person you are and how you could contribute to the company. Storytelling is one of the most powerful ways people have communicated throughout history; the stories you tell will make the interviewer remember you long after the interview is over.

# Example of a START Success Story

Read this sample success story and see how it demonstrates this person's problem-solving skills, initiative, and team building. She also offers some very concrete examples of how her actions benefited the organization.

## Situation

"In my first job, I worked at a small consulting company. Our department's job was to do basic research for companies that made products for consumers. All the people working in the department were statisticians, economists, or people who just loved working on a computer. We stayed in our own offices all day long and rarely interacted with each other."

## Trouble

"Being one of the newer employees, I wanted to learn as much as I could as fast as I could, so I got in the habit of stopping by other people's offices and asking them about their work. To my amazement, I found out that no one had any clue what anyone else in the department was working on. What was worse was that I realized we were often struggling to solve the same problems and reinventing the wheel every time—repeating the collection and analysis of data that someone else had already done for another client!"

## Action

"I compiled information about everyone's projects as I did my visiting and then wrote up a newsletter every two weeks."

## Results

"It wasn't long before people were telling me that they were using the information from the newsletter all the time. Before starting a project, they would check the newsletter to see what they could 'borrow' from past projects. This greatly reduced duplication of effort and saved time, so we were able to get more work done."

## Transferable Skills

"These are skills that I can bring to you as a project manager. I like things very organized. If I see something that needs to be done, I do it—I don't wait to have it officially made part of my job."

# measuring results

## Talk about your successes in concrete ways

Your success stories are a powerful way to illustrate your skills, abilities, and character. They also answer an interviewer's critical question: What can you do for our company? Your stories do this by describing how you have contributed to your past employers.

But beware! Don't fall into the trap of just talking about what you did in your past jobs or what your job responsibilities were. Talk about how the organization benefited as a result of your actions. It's the difference between saying "I was in charge of writing a newsletter" and saying "As a result of starting this newsletter, duplication of effort was eliminated, we saved time, and we could get more work done."

You can also make a more powerful impression by **quantifying** the scope of the outcome. "We could get more work done" sounds good. But "We were able to complete five more projects per week" sounds even better! Quantifying results offers "proof" that your outcomes actually occurred and shows you understand how your actions affected the company.

When you hear yourself talking about your actions or job responsibilities, ask yourself, "What does that mean to this company?" Put them in the context of how specifically they can help this employer. If you've been known for your great sales pitch, talk about how you can develop a similar pitch to sell this company's products.

What if you don't actually have the hard data on how an action you took improved productivity? That's okay. Just make a conservative assumption and tell the interviewer. For example, "By starting a task-sharing committee, we were able to get more work done. If we each took on only one more project per week, that meant we each tackled forty more projects per year!"

Employers love hearing that you helped save or make money. Look at your action and ask, "How did this help the bottom line?" If your action did not necessarily benefit the company's finances, focus on its other benefits.

**RED FLAG**

If the phone isn't ringing in response to the résumés and cover letters you've sent out, see Chapter 9 for ideas about how to get things moving.

# Results and Measures

Struggling with figuring out what results your actions produced? Take a look at this list.

## Actions

These are good topics for success stories. Employers value these attributes/actions so pick situations where you . . .

## Results and Measures

It's okay to state these without numbers. But they're more powerful *with* numbers when you . . .

| Actions | Results and Measures |
|---|---|
| Solved a problem | Saved or made money |
| Organized a project | Reduced costs |
| Overcame an obstacle | Reduced uncertainty |
| Innovated or created | Increased profits |
| Identified alternatives | Improved customer satisfaction |
| Filled a need | Reduced turnover |
| Resolved a conflict | Improved morale |
| Capitalized on an opportunity | Reduced duplication |
| Responded to a crisis | Increased control |
| Broke a stalemate | Exceeded a goal |
| Faced a fear | Saved time |
| Challenged the status quo | Reduced turnaround time |
| Fostered collaboration | Increased the number of customers |
| Unified people | Achieved a goal |
| Bridged a gap | Reduced the number of errors |
| Created order out of chaos | Increased predictability |
| Created a vision | Increased accuracy |
| Learned new skills | Used resources more efficiently |
| Took a risk | Reduced absenteeism |
| Aligned people to a goal | Improved communication |
| Took on something without being asked | Reduced exposure/vulnerability |
| Did the right thing | Reduced response time |
| Improved the skills of others | Retained more customers |

# in closing

## Ending your phone call with panache

You've spent 30 minutes on the phone with the interviewer, and the conversation is drawing to a close. You've answered his questions brilliantly and are feeling very confident. Now you need to end the call on a positive note and be assertive about the next steps.

**Ask any lingering questions.** If you still have questions about the position or the company, now is the time to get them answered.

**Summarize the call.** Briefly go over what you talked about with the interviewer. "I'm glad I've had a chance to talk with you about how my background in customer service fits what you're looking for in an assistant director. I understand that you need someone to train staff in this area, and that is something I am highly qualified to do. I'm looking forward to talking with you further about this." Make sure to reiterate your interest in the position, reminding the interviewer of the skills you would bring to the job and what specifically you can do for the company if you are hired.

**Decide on the next steps.** The interviewer may say, "I enjoyed talking to you. I'll let you know soon what we decide." But you need to subtly push him to be more specific. For example, ask: "When should I expect to receive a call or e-mail from you about my candidacy?" If he is still vague, you can say, "If I haven't heard from you, I'll call you next Friday morning to check in with you."

**Verify the details.** Be sure to get the correct contact information from the person who just interviewed you, including the spelling of his name, his title, and his e-mail address.

**Be polite.** Repeat his name when saying good-bye, and thank him: "Thanks again, Bill, for taking the time to call me today. I'm looking forward to speaking to you again next week."

# ASK THE EXPERTS

### What is the best way to follow up on a phone interview?

As with face-to-face interviews, there's no one correct way. Ending the phone conversation with a clear next step ("I look forward to your call next Monday") helps. Then follow up as agreed. If you don't hear from the interviewer by a designated time, give him a few more days and then contact him. Be polite and enthusiastic. Don't let emotions such as aggravation show through. For example, "Hello, this is <u>First Name, Last Name</u>. I'm following up on a phone conversation we had last Friday afternoon about the sales position. I was wondering if you have started scheduling people for interviews in person. Could you tell me where you are in that process?"

### I've called the interviewer back twice now to check on my status. Both times, he's said he was too busy to talk and that he would call me back. What's going on?

He may be too busy. He may have been told to wait until the boss comes back from vacation to set up interviews. He may have lined up another candidate and you're a backup. The point is, any of these scenarios is a possibility. When you follow up, try not to cross the line between showing enthusiasm and becoming an irritation. Ask him when would be a convenient time for you to call back. You could also increase the value of your contact: Send him an article he may find interesting or e-mail him with an idea prompted by your conversation. If this still doesn't generate a return call, don't give up before asking, "Would it be best to assume I'm no longer a candidate?"

### I get so nervous talking to employers, even on the phone. What can I do?

There are many ways to manage your anxiety. First, the more you prepare, the more confident you'll feel. Tell friends about your worries: They can help you be realistic. Slow down your physical response to fear and anxiety by taking deep breaths. Getting oxygen to your brain can help you think more clearly so that you'll interview better! And smile when you are speaking on the phone: This makes you sound confident and bright.

# now what do I do?
## Answers to common questions

### I have very little work experience. What accomplishments can I talk about?

Successes from part-time work, school, family life, community involvement, or philanthropic service can powerfully demonstrate your ability to set goals, organize projects, overcome obstacles, or solve problems. Use the START format (see pages 16–17) to tell the success story, and follow it with a statement that specifies the skills, behaviors, or characteristics you used to be successful. It is perfectly fine that you learned and demonstrated these skills somewhere other than in the workplace.

### I can't think of a single success to talk about. What should I do?

Sometimes it's difficult to identify and talk about accomplishments. This is especially true for some women (who grew up hearing "Don't brag!") and for people from cultures that socialize individuals to be equal members of the group. If you are struggling to come up with success stories, ask people who know you. Most likely they will respond with a "Remember the time when you . . ." story. But for the rest of your professional life, start building a "pat me" file (so named by someone who collected letters of appreciation, e-mail with thanks, examples of her work, etc., to pull out for interviews— and for days when she needed a "pat" on the back!).

### My success involved getting a team to stop bickering and unite around a common goal. How do I quantify that outcome?

Sometimes figuring out results and quantifying them can be difficult. Linking your action to a positive financial impact may be a stretch. This is where creativity, within realistic boundaries, comes into play. Ask yourself, as a result of uniting the team:

■ Could the team achieve something (a goal, deadline, or outcome) that otherwise would not have happened?

■ Did the team positively influence other parts of the organization?

■ Did the team avoid a crisis or a problem?

**What are some of the questions I can expect when interviewing?**

There is really no limit to what employers might ask you. However, some of the more common questions for which you should prepare responses include:

How would your last employer describe you?

What characteristics do you admire in others?

What is your ideal work environment?

What do you think it takes to be successful at our company?

What is the most important thing you look for in a job?

What have you disliked most in your past jobs?

Are you more comfortable leading or following? Why?

Do you work better alone or as part of a group? Why?

How well do you perform under pressure?

Where do you want to be in five years?

What was your worst failure? Why? What did you learn from it?

How does this job fit into your career progression so far?

What concerns do you have about this company?

What type of manager do you prefer working with?

How do you handle criticism?

Why do you want to leave your current job?

Why should I hire you?

# now where do I go?

**WEB SITES**

**www.CareerJournal.com**

*The Wall Street Journal*'s career column, with great articles on all aspects of job hunting and interviewing.

**www.wetfeet.com**

Great Web site with books (electronic or printed) such as *Job Search 101: Communicating Effectively*, 2003 edition, and *Job Search 101: Networking, Interviewing, and Getting the Offer*, 2002 edition. The Web site also has many useful articles, such as "How to Handle Your First Round Interviews" and "How to Conquer Pre-Interview Jitters."

## Chapter 2

# preparing for an interview

# countdown to an interview

**Here's the game plan**

So, you've aced the screening phone interview and you now have an appointment for the real interview next Thursday. Terrific. Now what?

Prepare, prepare, prepare. Make a checklist of what you will need to say and bring. Many job seekers ignore this crucial step. They don't practice how they will answer difficult questions or they don't remember to bring a résumé for the interviewer who may have misplaced theirs at the last minute. Here's why you should prepare.

**It builds confidence.** Remember all the stress and anxiety you feel about interviewing? Much of that is fear of the unknown. You don't know what the interviewer will ask, or who she is, or whether she will like you. The more you prepare, finding out as much as possible about the company and practicing what you'll say in each possible scenario, the less uncertainty you'll have to worry about.

**It improves the likelihood of success.** Just as in sports, you have to build up your interviewing muscle and skill.

**It reduces the surprises.** A big source of anxiety is worrying about what the interviewer will do or ask. During preparation you will figure out what questions and actions you can most likely expect, so there will be fewer surprises.

**It prepares you to handle the curveballs.** There will always be questions that come out of left field. But with preparation, there will be fewer of them.

If a job opening generates 100 résumés, an employer generally will interview 5 to 10 candidates in person. You are all sprinting toward the finish line. Preparation can be your competitive edge.

# Countdown to Interview Day

| WHEN | | WHAT |
|---|---|---|
| **Right away** | ✓ | Prepare your answers for the typical questions. |
| | ✓ | Write down your success stories. |
| | ✓ | Select your references. |
| | ✓ | Learn about the organization and its people. |
| | ✓ | Prepare the questions you will ask the interviewer about the job and the company. |
| | ✓ | Select your outfit and have it dry-cleaned or laundered if necessary. |
| **1–2 days prior** | ✓ | Practice interviewing with a friend—have him or her ask you questions and practice your responses (you can also practice in front of a mirror or a videocamera). |
| **Day before** | ✓ | Call the company to confirm the appointment and get directions if necessary. If you do not have the exact title of the person you will be speaking with, make sure you get this now! |
| | ✓ | Practice getting there (this eliminates a great source of anxiety!) to figure out the directions and the timing. |
| | ✓ | Try on your interview outfit and check for loose buttons, hanging hems and threads, and stains. |
| **Night before** | ✓ | Lay out the clothes you will wear. |
| | ✓ | Pack up any material you will take with you to the interview. |
| **Day of** | ✓ | Eat a good meal! Even if the jitters make it difficult to swallow, it's important that you eat carbohydrates (fruit, cereal, bread) and protein (meat, cheese, eggs, peanut butter) to keep you energized all day! |

# check your references

## Select and manage them carefully

Now is the time to double-check your references. Before an interview, be sure that you have at least three solid references lined up. Employers use your references to:

- confirm what you say on your résumé and in the interview
- provide proof that you can do the job
- dispel any lingering doubts they may have about you
- tilt the hiring decision toward you rather than another candidate

Keep those functions in mind when selecting which references you want to give. You want to use those references that will help you get the job. Obviously, at least one former boss will be needed. If you have several to choose from, select the boss who supervised you on a job most like the one for which you are interviewing. Be creative with your references: If the new job calls for interpersonal skills, use community or religious leaders or people with whom you have done community or philanthropic work.

Some tips for helping your references help you:

**Give them a heads-up.** When asked for a reference, explain that you'd like to call that person first to let him or her know of the coming call. Tell your reference about the job and concerns/interests the employer may have.

**Follow up.** Check back with your reference in a week and ask if the employer revealed any concerns that you should follow up on.

**Show appreciation.** Drop your reference a thank-you note. And when you land that job, be sure to express your gratitude to the references who helped you seal the deal.

# **A**SK THE EXPERTS

### What if my job search goes on and on and my references wind up having to talk to multiple companies?

If a reference has been called three times, check in with her before using her name again. Offer the option of being removed from your list. If you explain your situation, she may agree to continue to support your efforts. Either way, thank her.

### What if I check with my references and find the prospective employer hasn't called?

Don't despair—that doesn't mean the employer isn't interested in you. References often aren't called. They are a formality that is ignored if time doesn't permit. You can go back to the employer, mention the situation, and ask if there is anything else you can do to help in the hiring decision.

### If I'm employed, who do I use as references for my current job?

If your boss knows you are looking for a job, feel free to use him. If you don't want him to know, tell your interviewer that you want to keep this confidential. In this case, you might ask a coworker or supervisor who knows you very well to provide a reference for you, as long as he agrees to keep it private.

# impressive material

## Ways to leave a lasting impression

You've crafted brilliant responses to questions, you've got your references lined up—what next? Be sure to bring material you can leave behind. Always carry several clean copies of your résumé in your briefcase or notebook. You never know when an interviewer might need one. If you have a business card, bring several of those.

Now consider anything that will showcase your work. These props can be anything from an ad campaign you worked on to a newsletter you were featured in to a finished product you helped create. Consider buying a three-ring notebook or folder with acetate sleeves and putting in examples of achievements. This "portfolio" can distinguish you from the pack, since most candidates don't bring in items. If you have extra copies of any of the material, you can leave them behind with the interviewer.

Here are some things you might include as "proof" of your accomplishments.

- thank-you letters from clients
- "job well done" e-mail from the boss
- certificates of achievement
- awards and plaques
- performance appraisals
- photos of awards ceremonies

It is also a good idea to show an example of your writing. Writing is a critical skill in most jobs, so show off your abilities with brochures, articles, or reports you've written. (Take care to select pieces that don't violate confidentiality.) Include a few samples in your portfolio.

# Getting to the Interview

Believe it or not, finding the location of your interview can be a huge source of stress. Don't lie in bed the night before your interview worrying about missing street signs or changed bus routes. Check the route out the day before. Try these other stress relievers.

**Get directions.** When you get the call for the interview, ask for directions. If you forget to ask, you can always call back and obtain directions from the receptionist or phone operator. Company Web sites also frequently include directions.

**Use the Internet.** There are many Web sites that allow you to type in your starting point and desired destination to produce a detailed travel guide. Some of the more popular ones are www.mapquest.com, www.mapblast.com, and http://maps.yahoo.com.

**Take a test run.** The best-intentioned receptionist could still be off by one wrong turn. Don't wait until it's too late to find out that she sent you off in the opposite direction.

**Get the timing right.** On that test drive, determine how long it will take you to get to your interview. Keep in mind the effect rush hour may have on your timing. Add in an extra half hour—detours, traffic accidents, and wrong turns can easily eat those extra minutes up, and you don't want to be late.

Sometimes you can't help being late. As soon as you know you're going to be late to an interview, call. Ask if they'd still like you to come in or if it would be more convenient for them to reschedule.

# presenting yourself

**Your choices say
a lot about you**

Your interview day is finally here. Wonderful! You've had a nourishing meal and you're ready to get dressed. Naturally, you have already made sure that you don't need a haircut and that your favorite jacket isn't missing a button. How you present yourself is too important to be determined at the last minute.

Some guidelines for choosing what to wear:

**Conservative rules the day.** You want to wear something that makes the interviewer think "professional" and "competent." You also want to choose something that avoids directing the focus away from you and onto your clothes.

**Grooming counts.** An expensive suit will not compensate for dirty fingernails, messy hair, and wrinkled clothes. Good grooming indicates attention to detail and respect for others.

**Fit in to stand out.** Ideally you want your outfit to fit in with what other people will be wearing. The challenge is figuring out what the organization's "dress code" is. You can do this in several ways. Watch people as they enter the building from the parking lot. Look at photographs of employees on the company Web page or in its annual reports. Ask a friend who works in a similar profession, industry, or company.

**Err on the side of formality.** It's better to show up too formally dressed than too informally. Your aim is to be dressed slightly more formally than your interviewer.

**Go for the tried and true.** Select something that makes you feel good and is comfortable (particularly for long interview days). Don't wear something brand-new—halfway through the interview you don't want to find yourself limping around on blistered feet or trying to keep the scarf from slipping off your neck.

**Look professional, not provocative.** Don't overdo the perfume or aftershave. Makeup should be subtle. Your hairstyle should not overwhelm your face and should allow the interviewer to see your eyes. Limit the amount of jewelry you wear. You want the interviewer's attention focused entirely on your message.

# ASK THE EXPERTS

**I'm interviewing at a very high-powered firm. Should I wear my wedding ring to the interview? I don't want the interviewer to assume that because I'm married I won't want to work late or over the weekends.**

An interviewer may or may not make that assumption. But since there is no way to forecast her reaction, you may want to strategically decide whether to wear or display anything that makes an obvious statement about your lifestyle, religion, group or school affiliations, sexual orientation, nationality/ethnicity, or political beliefs.

**I have a small diamond stud in my nose. Is that okay for an interview?**

Leave it in? Take it out? While the choice seems easy, it's not. Your choices can reveal a great deal about who you are as a person and what you believe in. Consequently, it's very important for you to make a conscious decision about what you want to reveal to an interviewer, particularly in the early stages of the hiring process.

Answer these questions: Does this symbol represent an essential part of me that needs to be revealed now? Would revealing it later, on the job, cause others to lose their trust in me? Would it be impossible for me to do my job with this part of me suppressed? Does this symbol represent a private part of me that I don't plan on sharing in my professional life? Do I want to work for a company where this part of my identity would create static in the interview process? Am I using this as a test of this company's willingness to hire me or people like me?

Your appearance imparts a great deal of information to the interviewer. By understanding the choices you are making, you guide what she learns about you and how. There are no right or wrong decisions, no correct or incorrect choices. What is important is that you decide.

# while you wait

**Your interview begins the moment you walk into the building**

You made it to your interview on time and have been told to fill out a lengthy application. Whatever you do, don't slump down in a chair and start grumbling about it. Why? Because your interview has essentially begun. Everything you do from the moment you arrive can and will be counted for or against you. That's because interviewers are likely to hear about almost everything that goes on in the waiting room, be it from the receptionist or the mail attendant. So be careful what you do and say. Sure, you're nervous. The problem is that anxiety may show itself in unfortunate ways. Sometimes it can end your job hunt before you even meet anyone who might want to hire you.

## Take the Time to Fill Out the Application Carefully

**Make sure to:**

■ Write clearly, using block letters, and check spelling.

■ Be honest about why you left a job. "Reorganization" or "downsizing" sounds better than "laid-off" as explanations.

■ Come prepared with any information needed to do a background check on your credit, criminal record, and past employment.

■ Remember to sign and date it.

**And don't:**

■ Simply write "please see résumé." You need to supply all the details on the form because you are required to sign off on its accuracy.

■ Massage the truth by trying, for example, to pass off a relative as your former boss. Anything you write down is subject to verification. If you exaggerate just a little, this could lock you out of the job.

■ Become argumentative about having to fill out forms. You need to show the employer that you're willing to abide by his rules and that you're a team player.

# Pre-interview Manners

**Don't lose your cool.** One interviewer went home sick, meaning that another had to take on her workload. The candidates were given no explanation and were forced to wait. After 30 minutes, one applicant started pacing and scowling at the receptionist. The receptionist fired off a quick e-mail to tell the interviewer about this behavior, and when the applicant finally got into the interview, he got only five minutes, then was shown the door. The moral of the story: Stay calm, no matter what happens.

**Don't ignore the rules.** A candidate for a high-level job refused to fill out an employment application. After an administrative assistant explained its legal necessity to her, she ripped the application from the assistant's hands and sat down, banging her briefcase on the desk. After a few minutes, she returned a half-completed application. Clearly, she forgot that companies don't like obnoxious behavior and much prefer a show of a respect from someone who is ready to be a team player. Is it any surprise she never made it to round two?

**Don't be rude.** One recent college graduate became incensed when asked to take a typing test. "Do you think my parents put me through school just so I could be a typist?" he sneered at the receptionist. Grudgingly he took the test (after the computer was turned on for him) but the damage had already been done. His comments made everyone doubt whether he'd be able to deal politely with staff, customers, and vendors.

**Be patient.** When the receptionist told the candidate to have a seat and read some company literature while waiting, he rolled his eyes and sighed. He glared at his watch several times after he was told the interviewer would be with him shortly. The receptionist reported his behavior to the interviewer. He was given a short interview and never got called back. Obviously, he didn't get that manners are crucial in the business world.

# tests

**Psychological, drug, and skill evaluations: They can all be part of the screening process**

Testing has become the norm in most large companies, so don't be surprised if you are asked to take a test while you wait for your interview. There are five major types of tests. Which ones you will be asked to take depend on the requirements of the job.

**Drug tests**  Federal law requires that some employers, such as transportation companies, test prospective employees for drug use. Other companies use drug testing as a condition of hiring and continued employment. The most common testing method is urine sampling.

**Skills tests**  You may be asked to demonstrate the skills needed on the job by taking writing, typing, and computer software tests. Approximately 60 percent of employers use skills tests of some kind.

**Personality tests**  These tests provide a profile of your personal characteristics, assessing such things as adaptability, flexibility, creativity, and/or control of temper.

**Aptitude tests**  These tests measure reasoning, mathematical, writing, or verbal skills. While skills tests determine whether you can perform the job now, aptitude tests determine whether or not you can be trained to do the job in the future.

**Honesty tests**  These tests have arisen from employers' concerns about employee theft. The tests are administered when employees handle money, merchandise, or customer accounts.

# Preparing to Be Tested

**1. Know the industry standard.** If you are applying to a company that conducts interstate commerce, then expect to take a drug test. If you are applying to a large retail chain, then expect to take an honesty test.

**2. Find out about the company's stance on testing.** Some companies, for example, make drug testing a condition of hiring and continued employment. If you are applying for a job at such an organization, the company's policy should be clearly stated in such places as its Web site and other employment materials.

**3. Expect to take tests if you are applying to work for a large corporation.** The monetary costs of buying, administering, and getting professionals to read and interpret test results are high. Consequently it is the large multinational corporations that tend to use tests. In contrast, small employers are less likely to test, except where mandated by law.

**4. Ask about the connection between the test(s) and the job**—by law there must be a clear connection. If HR cannot explain the linkage, then red flags about this organization should go up for you. Well-run organizations tie the tests, particularly the personality, skills, and honesty ones, directly to the attributes of their top performers. The HR folks administer the test to one particular category of employees and create a profile of how the best employees in that job category score on the test. When you take the test, HR compares your score to their best performers.

**5. Check into how HR protects the confidentiality of the test results.** By law, the results may not be shared with another company or unauthorized employees.

**6. You may refuse to take a test**—and that's probably the end of your application. If federal or state laws require drug testing, then obviously you must submit to the process. If the organization has a clear policy on testing, then once again you must submit to the process if you want to be hired. Employers must give the same test in the same manner to all applicants who apply for the same job. Obviously, you cannot be the exception in such a situation.

# your interview demeanor

## Err on the side of formal and polite

Okay, you've filled out your application form and taken the required tests. Great. Now, finally, your name is called and your interview is about to begin. Take a deep breath. You have prepared for all of this, and you will do just fine.

Just one more thing: Mind your manners. If you're faced with an interviewer who is very informal and starts calling you by a nickname halfway through, stick to basic good manners and use her last name or ask permission to use her first name. While you don't necessarily need to maintain a stiff upper lip, it's better to err on the side of being overpolite rather than accidentally offending the interviewer.

Why is this important? During an interview, the screener is not just trying to figure out whether you have certain job skills. She is also trying to determine what kind of person you would be to work with, and this is the kind of information that will be passed on to a potential employer. Screeners make the assumption that what you do in the interview is what you'll do on the job. If you're polite in the interview, they assume you'll be polite on the job. Don't miss this easy way to score points!

## FIRST PERSON SUCCESS STORY

### Overcoming my nerves

I have always been shy in social settings, especially that first time when you meet someone at a party. I get so nervous I usually forget the person's name, which makes me so upset I clam up. When I mentioned this to my friend Mike, he suggested I try a little memory trick. As soon as you hear the person's name, associate it with something special about him. For example, Mike uses gel to spike his hair, so the memory trick is Mike the Spike. I used the same trick when I started interviewing. It worked like a charm. I could remember the person's name and use it when asking my questions about the job.

—Sam M., New York, New York

# Minding Your Ps and Qs

No matter who's interviewing you, make sure to follow these basic rules of etiquette.

**Stand up** whenever anyone enters or leaves the room and wait for them to sit before doing so yourself.

**Extend your hand for a handshake.** Grasp the interviewer's entire hand, not just his fingers. Have a firm but not painful grip. Pump his hand; don't just hold it.

**Permit the interviewer to introduce himself first.** That allows him to set the tone (formal or informal) for the meeting and clarifies what he wants you to call him (Mr., Ms., or first name).

**Repeat his full name.** Don't shorten it or use a nickname. "I'm pleased to meet you, _____." Then introduce yourself, using your complete name.

**Make good eye contact.** In American culture this signals respect.

**Accept offers of water and coffee,** unless you are afraid you'll spill it. Offering and accepting drinks sets a collegial tone and affirms the interviewer as the host.

**Open the door for your interviewer,** whether male or female, if you reach the door first.

**Do not smoke or chew gum** even if the interviewer invites you to do so.

**Turn off** cellular phones or pagers.

**Do not interrupt your interviewer** as he speaks or asks a question. Show that you are a good listener.

**Do not look at your watch.**

**Do not use slang, talk too much, tell jokes, or argue.**

# now what do I do?

## Answers to common questions

### Now that so many companies have dress-down policies and casual Fridays, I'm confused about what to wear to an interview. Any advice?

The goal is to come across as the consummate professional: well groomed, clean, crisp, and efficient. Therefore, it's always better to end up dressing a little too formally rather than too informally.

Men should stick with a suit and tie, worn with an ironed shirt. Don't overdo it on the cologne. Make sure your shoes are shined. Your face should be freshly shaved, or if you have a beard or mustache, it should be well trimmed.

Women should wear a business suit or tailored dress, stockings, and low heels. Keep perfume and makeup light and jewelry low-key. Nails should not be overly long. Stay away from garish nail polish. Bring just a small handbag and a briefcase and leave any extra bags at home.

### One of my references told a prospective employer that my excessive absenteeism is the reason I was fired. What can I do to prevent this from cropping up during my next interview?

There are a couple of things you can do. You might decide not to use that person as a reference, or you might explain the situation to an interviewer ahead of time. The best thing to do is be matter-of-fact about it: Explain that your last job did not work out because you missed too much work. Then be honest about the reason: "I was taking a real estate course at night" or "I was taking care of my sick father." Try to emphasize that your mind-set is now completely different, and that you have either taken care of the problem or firmly believe this new job will challenge you and keep you interested. You need to make sure the interviewer understands that coming to work every day, and even staying late if necessary, will not be a problem for you.

### I am worried that my past manager's reference won't be positive. What can I do?

Some employers will want to speak to your current or most recent manager. If you anticipate that this manager may have some negative things to say about you, it's important to prepare the interviewer with some brief neutral remarks: "My last manager and I had a difference in work style." Then describe that style, emphasizing that it was totally different from the target company's style: "He was very laid-back, and I like to run a tighter ship." Put a positive spin on the story.

Even if you had a terrible relationship with your boss, most likely he will not fill your interviewer's ears with horror stories. Most ex-bosses will confirm only that you did work there, for how long, and with what title. Going beyond that puts them at legal risk for defamation. For that reason, many ex-bosses won't even talk to interviewers and instead forward their calls to human resources to confirm employment data.

## now where do I go?

### WEB SITES

The Riley Guide: Interviewing
**www.rileyguide.com/interview.html**

Business Etiquette in the Job Search
**http://cba.uiuc.edu/general/jobs/search/etiq.html**

Etiquette in the Job Search: Mind Your Manners
**http://career.boisestate.edu/etiquette.html**

Guide to Business Etiquette
**www.careerservices.swt.edu/Student_Alumnus/JobSearchManual/Guide_to_Business_Etiquette.htm**

CollegeGrad.com
**www.collegegrad.com**
Contains useful information for people seeking entry-level jobs. Read the section on pre-employment testing to gain insight into the types of tests employers might use to make hiring decisions.

Nolo: Law for All
**www.nolo.com/lawcenter**
Offers a wide range of articles and documents on legal issues. There is a section on employment law, with a subsection on pre-employment testing. There is also a list of articles useful to both employers and employees.

**The following sites focus on the rights of workers. Use them for research if you feel you've experienced pre-employment discrimination.**

The National Workrights Institute
**www.workrights.org**

The American Civil Liberties Union
**www.aclu.com**

### BOOKS

**The Amy Vanderbilt Complete Book of Etiquette**
by Nancy Tuckerman and Nancy Dunnan

**Essential Business Etiquette: Bottom Line Behavior for Everyday Effectiveness**
by Lou Kennedy

**The Etiquette Advantage in Business: Personal Skills for Professional Success**
by Peggy Post and Peter Post

Chapter 3

# overview
# of an interview

# be observant

## Notice revealing details about the company

Before you even sit down with the interviewer, you can learn a lot about a company, and what to expect in the interview, just by being observant. As you make your way to the interview room, paying attention to details about the building and the staff you encounter can give you some valuable hints about the company's corporate culture and its basic rules of interaction.

Some things to notice:

**Parking lot:** Are there reserved spaces for the president and vice presidents? If so, this may tell you that hierarchy is important in this company. You may expect a longer interview process, not meeting the senior decision-makers until you've passed through more junior people first.

**Lobby:** What does the decor in the lobby tell you? Is it formal or creative and playful? The tone of your interview may mirror the tone set in the lobby. What's on the walls of the lobby? Every item is a window into what's important to the company. Often you'll find valuable information about the company (such as its mission statement or displays of its products) on the walls.

**Who greets you:** Who comes to meet you in the lobby? Is it the person with whom you have the interview or an assistant? That says a lot about the structure of the company. Formal companies will have you greeted by an assistant; in less formal firms, the hiring manager may be the one to greet you.

How does this person greet you? Does she address you formally or casually? Whichever way she talks, follow suit.

**Once inside the space:** What do you see as you walk down the hall? Are most people in cubicles with only the senior people in offices? This gives you an idea about hierarchy. How permanent are the names on the doors? Are there nameplates or just pieces of paper tacked to the door?

# ASK THE EXPERTS

## What exactly is "corporate culture" and how do I let an interviewer know I can adapt to it?

"Corporate culture" is shorthand for "the way we do things around here." It reflects the organization's underlying values, such as "change is good," "every man for himself," or "teamwork is key."

One way you can show an interviewer that you can adapt to a company's culture is to quickly observe the organization's unwritten rules and follow them. Another way is to choose success stories (see pages 16–17) that demonstrate rules and values similar to those of the company. In a highly informal company with strong personal bonds among employees, you may want to describe yourself as sociable and eager to interact with employees in informal contexts because that is where some of the best solutions to work problems arise. For example, mention an instance in which a novel approach to a problem may have arisen during a watercooler discussion. In a more formal corporate culture, be sure to highlight your ability to work independently and follow the rules, and stress your professionalism when dealing with clients.

## I interviewed with an organization that was into using titles and not names. What does this reveal about the company?

It sounds as if hierarchy is important to this organization's corporate culture, so make sure to be extra respectful of the senior executives you meet. When answering questions about working with others, you may want to stress that you follow directions well, respect authority, and always learn from more senior employees. You don't want to present yourself as dismissive of hierarchy by highlighting cases in which you went over the heads of senior staff to get a job done. You can also emphasize your desire to work your way up the ladder through concerted effort and concrete results.

# the interview process

## Know what to expect when you walk through the door

Be forewarned—the job interview process varies widely from organization to organization! Most job candidates, however, are put through multiple rounds of interviews. Since each organization has its own procedures for choosing new employees, ask the HR representative early on about the hiring process.

In many organizations, round one is with the HR screener. The purpose of this round is for the HR screener to ascertain your strengths and skills in comparison to those of the other candidates.

The HR screener often conducts round one as a telephone interview (see Chapter 1). Some organizations require that you state your salary needs during round one before your name can be forwarded to the hiring manager. The purpose of the salary screen is to align your expectations with the resources of the hiring organization.

The second round-three interviews will probably be a long day of meetings with your future boss, peers, and subordinates. Expect a wide range of questions, since people from different levels in the organization will have different views about the role for which you are applying. In the hopes of bringing some objectivity to the hiring process, large organizations, such as major banks, often train their hiring managers in behavioral interviewing methods (see pages 80–81).

Some organizations conduct round-three interviews. If you haven't already met the director or your boss's boss, you probably will now. If you still haven't been specific about your salary requirements, expect to spend considerable time discussing this topic.

Regardless of whom you are meeting and how long the process goes on, you must maintain your energy and focus through all the interviews. You never know who is going to have the final say in the hiring decision; it can turn on something as insignificant as an offhand comment to a receptionist.

# Basic Interview Rules to Live By

**1. Be cautious with humor.** This is not the place to tell jokes or poke fun at people. Don't even use self-deprecating humor (such as, "I couldn't please my boss if my life depended on it"). You want to build yourself up, not tear yourself down.

**2. Be positive.** Yes, you've had some bosses who were jerks, been treated unfairly in the past, or worked in some impossible conditions. Rather than talking about all the negatives, talk about the positives. Focusing on negatives raises a red flag for hiring managers. Instead, talk about what you learned from those situations and how you overcame those challenges.

**3. Avoid getting personal.** Stay away from topics such as the interviewer's family, relations with the boss or other employees, physical appearance, religious or political beliefs, age, and ethnic background.

**4. Be open-minded.** Even if you know you're the perfect candidate for the job, don't boast about it to the interviewer. Organizations look for employees who are respectful.

**5. Don't exaggerate or stretch the truth.** You want to present yourself in the best light, but be careful that everything you say can be backed up. For example, if a project was a team effort, talk about what you did. Don't take full credit.

**6. Control nervousness.** Discover where your nervous energy goes (laughing, playing with your jewelry, wringing your hands) and try to control it. If hands are the problem, try to keep them folded on your lap. If nervous laughter is a problem, role-play the interview process with friends until you can do it straight-faced. The interviewer expects you to be somewhat nervous, but don't let physical tics become distracting.

# the fundamental questions

**Employers have basic questions . . . and so should you**

During an interview, employers will ask you *tons* of questions about your education, past jobs, and skills. And they may ask these questions in a variety of different formats. No matter what shape an interview takes, however, there are really only three fundamental questions at stake:

- Do you have the skills to perform this job?

- Are you motivated to do the work?

- Would we like working with you, and will you fit into our organization?

Meanwhile, you should have fundamental questions for yourself as well. As you go through the interview, ask yourself:

- Do I have the skill set that matches the requirements of this job?

- Will I look forward to going to work each morning and doing the required tasks?

- Will I like working with these people?

Answering both your own fundamental questions and those of your employer requires a two-way conversation. Stay actively engaged in the conversation and think of ways to ask your questions directly and indirectly. Although there is no precise rule, you should probably be doing about 60 percent of the talking. If you are talking 90 percent of the time, something is wrong. If the interviewer is doing 90 percent of the talking, then something is *really* off.

So, remember both the employer's three fundamental questions and yours, and figure out ways to answer them, no matter what kinds of twists and turns your interview takes.

# Inspired Responses

## "So what do you do in your present job?"

**Uninspired response:** "As manager of accounts receivable, I manage three clerks, keep the books current, and flag accounts that are later than three months old." (All you did was describe your job duties, something they can read off your résumé.)

**Great response:** "As manager of accounts receivable, I focused my energy and perseverance on reducing the number of delinquent accounts. By setting goals, training my staff of three, and working with accounts to set up creative payment solutions, we were able to reduce the number of old accounts by 30 percent in my two years as manager." (Here you mentioned the skills you used to make an impact.)

## "Teamwork is a big part of our company. Have you ever been on a team where some members didn't pull their weight?"

**Uninspired response:** "Yes, I've been on teams like that. But what can you do? I just try not to let those people bother me." (This shows you simply accepted a negative situation and didn't try to change it.)

**Great response:** "Yes, I've been on teams like that. But I believe there are only very few people who actually want to freeload. Most people want to do a good job and make a decent contribution. I see it as a challenge to figure out what's holding a team member back. Were all his ideas ignored in the planning process? I try to figure out the problem so that I can turn the person around." (This response shows initiative, rather than mere acceptance of the situation.)

## "What are you hoping to achieve in your next job?"

**Uninspired response:** "I want to work with new people in new areas. I just need something completely different." (This answer is too vague to be of use.)

**Great response:** "After six years in customer service, I want to gain experience on the other side of the consumer pipeline: sales. My skills in building relationships and solving problems are directly applicable to this sales position, but now, instead of using them to keep customers satisfied, I'll get to use them to bring new customers in." (This answer is focused on what this new job is all about.)

# speaking their language

**You need to become multilingual**

English isn't the only language being spoken in an interview. For that matter, neither are Spanish, Chinese, or the other languages that are becoming widespread in the United States. But regardless of which language you speak, there are three other languages that are being "spoken" anytime you are with an interviewer:

**personal language:** your personal style of speaking, such as how fast or slow you speak, how directly (to-the-point) or indirectly you speak, how much you focus on people or on activities

**job language:** the jargon that is used by people in a particular job (accountant, marketer, project manager, etc.) and industry (medical, education, retail, etc.)

**body language:** messages conveyed by your face, eyes, hands, and posture

**You can increase your chances of a job offer by:**

**being aware** that these different languages exist

**learning to recognize** how your interviewer speaks these languages

**"translating"** your message into the interviewer's language

Just as a person who understands only English and a person who understands only Spanish will walk away from a conversation feeling bewildered and disconnected, so will two people who are speaking different personal, job, or body languages. It's easy to misinterpret someone who is speaking a different language or to label him negatively. And it can be easy to feel uncomfortable with him.

The more you can speak the languages of your interviewer, the more he will understand you and feel connected to you, and the more likely he is to think you would fit in. And naturally, this means it's more likely he will want to offer you the job.

# Personal Language: Speak to Be Heard

*Sometimes, but most likly Possibly.*

A powerful but subtle way of connecting with the interviewer is to recognize and use his personal language; in other words, mimic his particular way of speaking, including vocabulary, speed, and tone. So how do you identify your interviewer's language?

**Look at his environment.** If there are lots of family pictures, then revealing some information about your personal life may be appropriate, such as what part of the city you live in or what you like to do to relax. If the walls are covered with diplomas and certificates of achievement, then talking about your own awards and successes may be the best route.

**Observe the pace of his speech.** Does he speak quickly or slowly? With many details or just generalizations? You would do well to mirror his pacing. Does he look impatient or interrupt you when you are speaking for more than a minute or giving details? If so, shorten your responses.

**Listen for some key words.** Your interviewer will unconsciously expect you to use similar words. Does he talk in absolutes (such as "always" and "never") or in more guarded terms (such as "sometimes" and "possibly")? Does he talk in superlatives (such as "best," "greatest," "worst")? If your interviewer's language is peppered with "greatest" and you say your accomplishment was "pretty good," he could easily misinterpret your success story as just "okay" or even "not great."

# using the right job lingo

**Speak to show expertise**

**W**hether you're interviewing to be a restaurant manager or a software developer, one powerful way to demonstrate your qualifications for a position is to use the job's jargon, the special vocabulary or expressions spoken by people in a particular job function or industry. Some guidelines when doing so:

**Use job language correctly.** If you are not familiar with a term, don't use it. And if a term the interviewer uses is unfamiliar, don't try to pretend—this will only make you look worse if it comes out later that you have no idea what she's talking about. Ask for clarification.

**Ascertain your audience's language.** Make a mental note of terms your interviewer uses frequently, and use them in your responses. Using job language that your interviewer doesn't understand can hurt you if, as a result of it, she sees you as pompous and arrogant. If you want to get an idea of the language used by an organization ahead of time, check its Web site or corporate materials for hints.

**Use common business jargon.** This shows that you recognize that the entire reason for hiring you is to produce some output and to help the organization meet its goals. While you don't want to go over the top and sound like an infomercial for a management training course, you do want to establish your familiarity with accepted business ideas.

# Common Business Terms

Before your interview, you might want to familiarize yourself with the terms listed below and practice using them in different sentences. This will show that you grasp essential business concepts.

**Output, deliverables:** what you are being hired to produce. Example: "My output in past jobs has always been tied closely to the customer's needs."

**Return on investment (ROI):** how your output is measured against the cost of the resources that were invested in your effort. Example: "The return on investment for this project that I completed was 25 percent higher than the original estimate."

**Learning curve:** your process of learning the new job and the time it takes for you to become productive. The shorter, the better. Example: "Because of my past experience in this area, you can expect my learning curve on this job to be very short."

**Skill sets:** Every job usually requires a certain set of skills. For instance, a manager needs to have organizational and leadership skills. A computer programmer needs technical and problem-solving skills.

**Metrics:** measurements of how productive you are. They can be task-related (quality, quantity) or people-related (morale, turnover). The bottom line is the ultimate financial metric: Did the company make money (**profit**), lose money (**loss**), or come out even (**break even**)? Example: "I improved the bottom line for this division two months ahead of schedule, which contributed to a 50 percent increase in our profit by the end of the year."

# setting the right tone

## Using verbal and non-verbal cues for impact

Think about it: Your employer is going to spend more time with you each workday than with her partner, family, or best friend. So even if she's impressed with your résumé and your success stories, in the end what she really wants to know is whether she'll enjoy working with you.

Besides using job language and the interviewer's language for maximum impact during the interview, be aware of not just what you say but how you say it. And pay attention to the signals you send through your body language. All of these cues add up to a complete picture of who you are and play a crucial role in an interviewer's unconscious perception of whether you're the right one for the job.

Some basic guidelines:

**Be positive.** Talk about successes and refer to challenges as opportunities. Make sure to give recognition to others for their support in your successes, and make it clear that you view mistakes as ways to learn. Be honest about your past, but do not be naive. Put a positive (or, at worst, neutral) spin on anything in your background that may give an interviewer pause.

**Be specific. Vagueness can be off-putting.** State your goals clearly and offer specific examples of how you've used your skills in different situations. Be straightforward and concise about your strengths and weaknesses.

**Be low-maintenance.** Don't make the interviewer do all the work. Initiate small talk at the beginning, and put the interviewer at ease by asking her questions. Segue into your conversation.

**Be interesting.** Talk about unique or unusual things in your background. If you put the interviewer to sleep, she won't know what a terrific employee you'd be!

# Reinforce Your Verbal Message with Body Language

Your body language can also powerfully influence the interview process—for better or worse. Your body can hurt you by:

- distracting from your verbal message, so they don't hear you.
- contradicting your verbal message, so they don't believe you.

Research has shown that only 7 percent of the total meaning of your message is communicated through the actual words you use. Your face and body accounts for 55 percent of your message, and your voice accounts for the remaining 38 percent.

| Positive message: | Negative message: |
|---|---|
| **Face** | |
| Interested expression | Blank expression |
| Some facial animation | Avoidance of eye contact |
| Good eye contact | Rapid eye blinking |
| **Voice** | |
| Audible volume | Mumbling, low volume |
| Clear enunciation | Rapid pace |
| Energy (expression) in voice | Monotone |
| **Body** | |
| Erect posture | Slouching or lounging |
| Both feet on floor | Bouncing leg or foot |
| **Hands** | |
| In lap when resting | Playing with objects |
| Some slow gestures | Overly rapid gestures |

**Making it happen . . . or not**

Practice.
Get feedback from others.
Watch yourself in a mirror.
Eliminate things you know you play with: Keep hands empty, don't wear jewelry, and pull your hair back.
Take deep breaths to slow down your body's nervous response.

# handling curveballs

## Manage them well and score points

Sometimes during an interview, questions or situations may arise that take you off guard. For example, you're asked for your salary requirements within the first two minutes of the interview. The interviewer pulls his chair a little too close for comfort. You're told you don't appear qualified. There's no need to panic—you've just been thrown a curveball.

Some things you can't prepare for, but you can learn some general strategies for handling the unexpected. Your goal is to slow the situation down and to move on from the situation in the most face-saving way for both you and the interviewer.

**Repeat the question.** This is a time-honored tactic used by many professionals. Whenever you are asked a question (whether you know the answer or not), first repeat it before giving your response. This repetition helps you in several ways:

**1.** It buys you some time to think.

**2.** It allows you to slightly rephrase the question into something you can answer. For example, if the interviewer exclaims, "I don't see how you think you can do this job without any experience in this field," you could restate it as, "It sounds like I need to explain what I've learned in my past jobs that will help me in this management position."

**3.** It shows the interviewer that you are listening to him.

**Ask a question.** If the interviewer says, "Tell me about your computer skills," and you have few, you might reply, "It sounds like that's an important part of the job. Does your company offer computer training to its employees?" This is also a good strategy if you are asked a question and you want to clarify what the interviewer's underlying concern is before responding.

**State the obvious.** Use humor and be honest. It's okay to say, "Wow, I need to think about that question."

# HAT IF

## What if the interviewer asks me for my salary requirements early in the discussion?

Avoid being the one to put the first salary figure on the table, particularly at the beginning of the interview process. If the number is too high, it can disqualify you. If it's too low, you'll find it difficult to negotiate for more. You could respond, "I'm open to negotiation. Can you tell me more about the job so I'll have a better sense of what might be fair?"

## What if I'm asked a question I don't have an answer for?

If you don't have a clue, rather than make something up, discuss a related issue or situation. For example, if he has described a situation and asked, "What would you do?," you could respond, "I've been in a similar situation, and this is what I've learned works best." Then list general principles you follow.

If the question borders on an illegal invasion of your privacy (see page 58), or if your answer may be damaging to your chances, you can refuse to answer it. Politely state, "I would prefer to not answer that question." Recognize that this may jeopardize your candidacy. Or redirect the question and try to get at the heart of the concern with a response like this: "If you are asking me how many children I have because you are worried about absenteeism, you should know that I have taken only two sick days in the last year at my current job."

## What if the interviewer states a negative observation about me?

No one wants to hear, "You're not qualified for this job." But such a comment may be valuable feedback. Maybe you aren't qualified and the interviewer's observation can save you the frustration of going after a job that isn't a good match.

He may also be revealing underlying concerns that you haven't addressed yet. Ask, "What do I need to be successful in this job?" This way, you can identify what information the interviewer needs that you haven't yet shared about yourself.

# illegal questions

## Questions they aren't allowed to ask

After countless hours of preparation, you're sitting with the interviewer and you're ready to amaze her with your brilliance. Great. But the first question out of the interviewer's mouth is, "So, where is your family from?"

Though state laws vary, employers are generally restricted from asking about your age, national origin, race/color, citizenship, disability, and criminal record. But that doesn't mean they won't try. The interviewer may not know any better, may want to see how you handle an uncomfortable situation, or may be improperly getting at a legitimate concern.

Most likely you'll be shocked, angry, or intimidated. And then you'll either refuse to answer (and feel righteous . . . while you're being shown the door), or answer (and feel angry . . . and wonder whether you'd even want to work for a jerk like that).

But wait—there is a third option: Attempt to answer the underlying concern that has been improperly probed. Behind many illegal questions is a concern about whether you can do the job or how you will fit in with the other people in the company. When answering a question that invades your privacy, make your best guess as to what the underlying concern may be and then relate your answer to job performance. For example:

**Do you plan to have children?** may reveal concerns about how long you would remain on the job. So your response could be, "I may or may not decide to have a family, but I can assure you that your investment in me will be well rewarded."

**Are you a U.S. citizen?** may reveal concerns about documentation. Your response could be, "I am authorized to work in the United States."

If you can't guess the possible underlying reason, ask. For example, "I'm not sure how that relates to the job. Can you clarify that for me?" Employers are allowed to ask only questions that relate to the job. Asking them to connect their questions to the job will not offend them, and this way you will be helping them stay within legal bounds.

# WHAT IF

### What if I'm asked, "Can you work for a boss who is younger than you?"

This is an illegal question that may reveal an underlying concern that, because of your age, you may not fit in with the company culture. The best response to a question like this would be, "I always learn a lot from my bosses and from other employees, no matter what their background. In my experience, the more diverse a boss's experience is from mine, the more I'm able to learn how to approach problems from different perspectives."

### What if I'm asked, "Are you married or planning to get married?"

The underlying concern behind this illegal question may be whether you would be willing to relocate or travel if this job required it. It may also be a question about whether you would be able to put in the occasional overtime this job may require.

The best response to a question like this would be, "I always do my best to separate my personal life from my job and to balance the demands they make on me. No matter what may be happening in my personal life, my commitment to my job remains unchanged. If there are periods where extra time or effort are required, I always do my best to contribute as much as possible."

### What if I'm asked, "Do you have any physical disabilities?" or "How is your health?"

The underlying concern behind these illegal questions may be whether you would be able to perform this job due to disability or health reasons. The best response to this would be, "I am well prepared to perform any of the tasks outlined in the job description."

### What if I'm asked, "When did you graduate from college?"

The employer is probably trying to pin down your age. You could answer, "While that was prior to 1980, I would like to underscore two things: my energy and vitality, which will help me greatly in this job, and my comfort level with professionals of all ages."

# inexperienced interviewers

**Don't let a poor interviewer hurt your chances of success**

You expect your interviewer to be professional and skilled. But in the real world the person who interviews you is often overworked, stressed out, and untrained. Your interviewer may be the hiring manager who's been trying to do both his own job and the vacated job. Or you may be facing a human resources manager who knows more about benefits than interviewing, or the hiring manager's assistant, who got this interview dumped in her lap 10 minutes before you arrived.

So how do you not let this person ruin your chance for a successful interview? Two strategies:

**State your case.** Your interviewer may not know the questions to ask. She may be shy and uncomfortable talking to strangers. But just because she doesn't ask you questions doesn't mean you can't tell her your success stories and all the great things you bring to this job.

**Manage the interviewer.** If she seems scattered, draw her in. If she is incessantly talking about herself, politely interrupt and insert information about yourself. Do whatever it takes to get her attention and win some floor time!

## FIRST PERSON SUCCESS STORY

### Pay attention!

After weeks of getting the runaround from the floor manager and staff at this little boutique, I networked my way into a meeting with the owner. I knew that once she heard some of my sales strategies, she'd find a way to hire me, even though she wasn't advertising any openings. The problem was that she was on and off the phone for the first 15 minutes of our appointment. When she hung up, I suggested she show me around her store. She loved the idea. Not only did she get to show off her operation, but she couldn't be interrupted by the phone. She invited me back for another interview the next day, and I suggested we do it after the store closed. She hired me the following week. I learned that when faced with a busy potential boss, it's a good idea to find a way to get her undivided attention.

—Susan F., Tampa, Florida

# ASK THE EXPERTS

### How do you get a word in edgewise when the interviewer is constantly talking?

The interviewer may be talking out of nervousness, lack of know-how, verbosity, or ego.

**Nervousness or lack of know-how:** A polite interruption may get you the floor. You could say, "Maybe you'd find it useful if I told you a little about myself." You can ask and answer your own questions. For example, "You may be wondering how my teaching experience would help me in this position. Let me address that . . . ."

**Verbosity:** Again a polite interruption, prompted by something he has said, may work. For example, if he has been rambling about all the crises he faces, you could jump in with, "I know what you mean. In one of my past jobs we also seemed to have crises all the time. Here's what I did about it. . . ."

**Ego:** Ask the interviewer questions about his area of expertise. You may score points because you are such a good listener! Another strategy is to ask, "Where does the interviewing process go from here?" That may get him either to focus on you or to set up an interview for you with the next person in the company.

### What should I do if the interviewer keeps bad-mouthing the company during the interview?

This is a good time to keep quiet and listen—don't even think of commiserating or sympathizing. You may also wonder whether you want to work for a company whose employees are so openly negative. Ask for interviews with some other people and put off drawing any conclusions until after you speak to them.

### What if the interviewer is constantly being interrupted or looking at his watch?

It is entirely possible that you have caught him at a bad time. A crisis may have arisen. Deadlines may be looming. It is perfectly polite to suggest that he reschedule the appointment. You could say, "It looks like there's a lot going on today. Would it be helpful to find a time for this interview when things have settled down?"

# your turn for questions

The interview process is a two-way street: Not only are you being interviewed, but you are interviewing the organization to see whether it really is the right place for you. So, before you go in for the interview, make a list of things you need to know. The answers will help you decide whether you want to continue the interview process. (And the questions also make you look really smart and motivated!)

Some examples of questions you might ask:

**What is it like to work here?**

- How long do people work here, and why do they leave?
- How do employees talk with senior management?

**What will my job responsibilities look like?**

- What are the major responsibilities of this job?
- What expectations do you have for the position?

**What support will I have in meeting job requirements?**

- What kind of budget is there for this department, and who determines it?
- What kind of administrative support is there?

**What kind of authority will I have?**

- Who would report to me?
- Who would be my supervisor?
- What decisions would I be able to make alone? With approval?

**How will my performance be evaluated?**

- How often would my performance be reviewed? By what process? By whom?
- If I do well, how might I be rewarded?

# "Red Flag" Answers

When you ask questions such as the following about an organization, certain answers can be a sign of underlying trouble.

**Question:** "Is there an open-door policy here?"

**Answer:** "We have a standard procedure for submitting queries to senior staff or requesting meetings."

This is probably a company built on hierarchy, not a friendly open-door style. Having a "standard procedure" means that the company probably does not welcome informal requests or knocks on the door. If you are someone who likes spontaneous, casual interaction among employees and prefers having an approachable boss who is open to new ideas and change, this may not be the place for you.

**Question:** "Who had this position before, and why did that person leave?"

**Answer:** "That is confidential information," or "The person was not performing as required," or "The person decided to work for another company."

If you receive any of these answers, chances are there was some controversy surrounding the last person's departure and that she either resigned or was fired. It could be that she wasn't cut out for the job, but it also can mean there are problems with this position. Try and probe further to find out what they are. Perhaps the workload was too heavy or the duties unclear, or it ended up being a dead-end job without the possibility of promotion, or the supervisor was difficult to work with.

**Question:** "Can you describe the coworkers for this position? What is their experience and length of time working here?"

**Answer:** "I'm not sure who is in this department," or "We recently hired a lot of new people and I'm still learning their names."

If your interviewer doesn't know who your coworkers would be, this could mean that either the interviewer truly doesn't know much about this department or there is a lot of turnover at this company. If you suspect that turnover is high, try to get at why this might be. You might rephrase the question to find out how coworkers support one another in getting the job done; perhaps there is an imbalance of tasks that is creating a stressful work environment.

# closing

**Last impressions count, too**

You've spent an hour together and you've answered all the questions perfectly. You feel like you've aced the interview. Time is up and you're feeling like you're home free! But there are still things you can do to proactively affect the interview process.

**Ask questions.** Toward the end of the interview, interviewers often ask, "Do you have any more questions?" Never say no! Always have a few good questions to ask at this point (even if it means holding some in reserve for just this moment).

**Review the information you've collected.** Have you gathered all the information you need to decide whether you want to proceed in this interview process?

**Clarify the next steps.** If the interviewer hasn't already done so, ask him to spell out what comes next. When can you expect notification? If you have not heard anything in a week, is it okay to contact the office?

**Make a persuasive closing statement.** This is the last thing the interviewer will hear you say. You want him to remember that:

- You have the skills for the job (so briefly summarize what you have to offer).
- You would fit in well in the organization (so list personal attributes that match the company's culture and needs).
- You want the job (so include what you've learned about the company and/or the job that has excited or impressed you).
- The company will benefit from hiring you (so explain what you will do for them).

Along with your success stories, prepare this statement in advance. It's too important to blow.

**Say thank you.** Make sure to thank and say good-bye to everyone you've talked with—even the receptionist.

# Savvy Closings

Before you go in for an interview, prepare and practice a sample close so that when the time comes you're ready to end the discussion confidently and memorably. Here are some samples to get you thinking.

**Example 1**

**Poor close:** "Thanks for talking to me today. I really enjoyed meeting you. I really do want this job, and I hope to hear back from you soon about it."

**Problem:** This is too vague; there is no reference to why you want the job and what skills you will bring to it, and no indication of when you will check back with the employer.

**Good close:** "After speaking with you today, I am very excited about the possibility of working for your company. The support your employees get for innovation is really terrific. Your quick pace and deadlines appeal to me as I work best under pressure. Once more, I've got the analytic skills, the teamwork skills, and the self-motivation to quickly get up to speed on the job and start creating products for your customers. I hope to hear from you this week about your decision, and if not, I will call you next Friday."

**Example 2**

**Poor close:** "So, when do I start?"

**Problem:** Some people actually think this is a humorous way of ending an interview and that demonstrating such spunk will shock the interviewer into answering, "Monday morning." It may have worked for a very few people, but most likely you'll just come off sounding arrogant or flippant.

**Good close:** "I enjoyed meeting you today and look forward to hearing from you soon about the next steps. If I haven't heard from you by May 1, I'll check back with you by e-mail as you suggested. I also want to reiterate how much I've enjoyed learning about the company's goals for 2003, and I want to remind you that during five years as a manager at my last job, I consistently increased my department's revenue by 20 percent each year, resulting in my department winning our company's annual sales award three years in a row. I'm ready to bring this talent to work for you as soon as possible."

# following up

## Stay on their minds once you're out the door

After the interview, keep in contact with the interviewer. This enables you to continue to influence the interview process, and reminds the interviewer of how courteous, respectful, and professional you are. Then, if you don't land this job, he may remember to contact you for future openings or give your name to someone in another organization or division in the company to consider.

A well-written thank-you letter, sent within 24 hours of your interview, can make the difference between getting a job offer or not. The letter should be typed or handwritten on your own clean professional stationery. Include a brief reiteration of the job as you understand it, points you may have forgotten to mention, and responses to any concerns expressed. Restate that you want the job and describe how you will follow up.

If you met with more than one person at a company, send a letter to each person who interviewed you. Customize each letter to reflect the conversation you had with that person (they may compare letters).

E-mail is not a substitute but can be an added form of thanks and should follow the standard letter format.

### Sending Follow-up Materials

After sending a thank-you letter, think of other ways to stay in touch. Sending interviewers information regarding a need, concern, or interest of theirs reconnects them to you and positively reflects on your good listening, problem solving, helpfulness, and follow-through.

Did the interviewer talk about a challenge the company is facing? E-mail him a Web site that examines that challenge. Did you promise you'd send him additional materials about yourself? Don't forget—and the sooner, the better. Did you talk about related work you've done for a vendor the company could use? Send the contact information.

375 Cranberry Lane
Church Falls, Ohio 54321
August 18, 2003

Ms. Leslie Paresky
Director, Human Resources
Mandolin Display Products
200 Turnpike Street
Lafayette, Ohio 54321

Dear Ms. Paresky:

I greatly appreciated the time we spent together yesterday discussing the product manager position. After hearing about Mandolin's "customer first" philosophy, I am more eager than ever to become a part of your organization.

As a result of our conversation, I feel I would be able to make a significant contribution in helping Mandolin meet its aggressive marketing targets. For the past five years while working at Dexter, I increased our customer base by 30 percent. I did this by developing strong relationships with our clients, solving their unique production needs, and developing a loyal customer base with high retention.

I have the interpersonal skills to make these connections with your customers, the analytic skills and creativity to create solutions for their problems, and the team-building experience to collaborate across Mandolin's workforce.

Once again, thank you for your time and interest. I will call you in two weeks to see if you have any other questions.

Sincerely,

*Alison Maxwell*

Alison Maxwell

**Annotations (right margin):**

- Your contact information
- Date
- The interviewer's name, title, and contact information
- Salutation with title
- Thank the person and indicate your interest in the position and why.
- Position yourself as meeting the company's needs. Include information about your personal attributes and background.
- If possible, connect your skills to what you can do for the company.
- Spell out the agreed-upon next steps.
- Closing
- Signature
- Your name typed

# now what do I do?

## Answers to common questions

### I hate leaving an interview and not knowing whether I will ever be called back. Can I ask about my chances?

Absolutely! Be respectful and polite and ask, "Could you tell me where I stand in the interview process?" or "As a result of our conversation here today, do you see me as a viable candidate?" An even better way to ask (because it gives you the opportunity to respond to the interviewer's concerns before you leave) is, "Do you see any barriers that would prevent me from moving ahead in this interview process?"

### If I think of a better way to answer a question after I gave my first response, can I go back and answer it again before my interview is over?

Definitely go back to the question and give your brilliant response. The interviewer will appreciate your effort to put your best foot forward. You could segue into your new response by saying, "If it's okay with you, I'd like to revisit your question about how I'd handle an irate customer. After thinking about it more, I think a better course of action would be . . ." This shows an ability to learn, a desire to improve, and a willingness to admit mistakes—all great attributes.

### I've called human resources several times and sent the interviewer a thank-you letter and a couple of e-mails, but I still haven't heard back from the organization. What's the fine line between showing interest and being a pain?

It is a fine line, and there's no set number of appropriate contacts. Your goal is to keep on their radar screen. It's easy to get angry or embarrassed by the one-way communication and stop. But consider this: In research of successful salespeople (and selling yourself is what you are doing), the differentiating characteristic was persistence. While the successful salesperson made an average of five attempts at the sale, the less successful salesperson quit after two. So don't give up too quickly—vary the way you contact the company and keep sending information of value, and you may find you get called in six months for a new position that has opened up.

### Persistence is fine, but when do I give up?

Don't give up without one of two things happening first. One, you could ask your contact whether you should give up. You could say, "I am obviously very interested in getting a job in your organization, but I don't want to take up your time if you think there is no future here for me. I'd appreciate you letting me know if I should keep contacting you." Usually your contact will be honest and say no or not at this time.

Two, you need to ask yourself, "Is this the best use of my time?" By contacting this organization, are you preventing yourself from aggressively going after other opportunities? If so, you need to give up on the organization.

## I've gone through what seems like 100 interviews with this one company. They just called for the 101st. When do I tell them to "fish or cut bait"?

It's up to you. Again, ask yourself, "Is going to this interview the best use of my time?" If it means you aren't pursuing other leads, then it isn't. The interview process also tells you a lot about the company. Analyze the interview process to help you decide whether you'd like to work there or not.

# now where do I go?

## Legal information on the Web:

FindLaw
**www.findlaw.com**

Legal Information Institute, Cornell Law School
**www.law.cornell.edu**
Search here for information about employment law.

JobWeb
**www.jobweb.com**
Articles on what employers can and can't ask.

## Free guidelines for permissible questions:

U.S. EEOC
Office of Communications
1801 L Street N.W.
Washington, DC 20507
Ask for "ADA Enforcement Guidance" (released in October 1995).

## Great periodicals for learning about employment trends:

**HR Magazine**
606 North Washington Street
Alexandria, VA 22314
703-548-3440

**Fast Company**
**www.fastcompany.com**
800-688-1545

**National Employment Business Weekly**
**www.nbew.com**
800-562-4868

**Chapter 4**

# interview styles

## Interview methods  72
Know the five styles of interviewing

## The conversational interview  74
Managing the casual chat

## The hypothetical interview  76
Handling "what if" questions

## The stress interview  78
Show you can handle the pressure

## The behavior-based interview  80
A way to predict your future job behavior

## The case question interview  82
Be prepared to think on your feet

## Now what do I do?  84
Answers to common questions

# interview methods

Be prepared to face the
new breed of interview

The fundamental questions of an interview (see pages 48–49) may be well hidden in any of a variety of interview methods. These methods range from unstructured to highly structured, with interviewers trained to give points for certain kinds of answers. Long gone are the days when a rambling chat about your hobbies would land you the job!

Chances are that you're likely to encounter one of several distinct interview methods designed to produce in-depth knowledge about your aptitude for the job. Which style you'll run into depends on the job you are applying for as well as the organization's own culture and style of decision making. During your job search, you need to be prepared to encounter any of these interview methods.

**The Conversational Interview,** which can seem like a casual chat, conceals a highly effective method of obtaining knowledge about your abilities.

**The Hypothetical Interview** peppers you with all sorts of "what if" questions to see how well you think on your feet.

**The Stress Interview** is used to find out how you respond to chaotic situations and deal with aggressive, critical, or off-the-cuff questions.

**The Behavior-Based Interview** assesses your behavior in past job situations, using it as a predictor of future success.

**The Case Question Interview,** often used by management consulting firms, tests your logic and problem-solving skills with brain teasers and hypothetical situations.

# ASK THE EXPERTS

### How do I know what style of interview I'll get?

You don't. There are, however, general guidelines. If you are interviewing at a large corporation, then the interviewers are likely to use behavioral interviews. Larger companies have the resources to employ more sophisticated interviewing techniques. If you are interviewing for a consulting position, then case questions are likely to be used.

During the first phone interview you might do two things to assess how your future interviews will be conducted in that organization. You can note what kinds of questions you are asked. If the interviewer asks you to talk about work situations from the past and the results, then expect a behavioral interview. During the phone interview, you may ask directly whether the organization has a specific method for interviewing. You might also want to look at the organization's Web site and see whether it discusses the interviewing process. If you know people inside the organization, you might ask them whether there are preferred procedures for interviewing people.

### I submitted a résumé for a job opening six months ago, and this morning they finally called me in for an interview. What does this mean?

The hiring process gives you excellent cues about how the organization is run. If you submitted a résumé for a position six months ago and are just now getting a call, then ask yourself what might be going on in that organization. Make sure you inquire about the delay in interviewing and hiring and ask yourself if the reasons provided make sense.

If, on the other hand, you submit a résumé and are called about it the next day, this is probably a dynamic, fast-moving organization in a rush to fill a crucial job. It could be that this position is a high-pressure, deadline-oriented job that must be filled immediately for the organization to run smoothly. If you are concerned about working under pressure, make sure to ask questions during the interview to learn more about the organization's work environment.

# the conversational interview

## Beware of the casual chat

Some organizations do not have a standardized way of interviewing candidates. Consequently, their employees interview candidates in a relaxed, conversational manner. If you enter an office and the interviewer starts chatting about the weather, then wants to know with whom you worked at your last job, you are in a loose, conversational-style interview. When the hour ends, you wonder, Was I even interviewed?

Yes, you were. Conversational interviews can easily become traps for candidates. If you go along with the style of the interviewer, then you may fail to talk about the job and your qualifications for it. On the other hand, if you take over the conversation, pushing your credentials and selling yourself aggressively, then the interviewer may think you are a control freak. Either way you lose. Your best bet is to find the middle ground, chatting with the interviewer and pulling the conversation toward the job and your qualifications. How should you do that?

First, recognize that your interviewer is conducting a conversational interview. If you are still chatting 15 or 20 minutes into an hourlong interview, then you are probably in a conversational interview. The second step is to tell the interviewer that you are very interested in the job and company. Ask him if you might turn the conversation to those topics. The trick is to turn the conversation to job-related topics in a collaborative way.

Occasionally, interviewers are setting another kind of trap. Some organizations need people who can create structure out of disorder. If this is true of this prospective employer, then the interviewer may be waiting to see how you respond to a disjointed conversation. Take the steps listed above. If that does not work, then name what you are experiencing in the interview. For example: "This interview feels like a casual conversation and I'm really enjoying it. But I would really like to get into the needs of the position in a little bit. I can be casual, but I'm also organized and task-oriented, and am hoping to be able to apply those skills in this job."

# Avoiding Personal Topics

**W**atch out! Sometimes an interviewer may simply seem to want to chat about your interests, but these questions can conceal underlying questions about how well you fit with an organization.

**Sample question:** "So tell me about your hobbies. What do you like to do in your spare time?"

**Sample response:** "I'm very committed to my work, so I usually don't have a lot of spare time. When I do have time to myself, however, I like to read, go shopping, and cook. In my last job, I took a personal interest in helping our customers and often ended up working overtime, so when I came home I usually just wanted to do something relaxing."

This question may be concealing a concern about whether your life outside work is more important to you than your job. This is not the time to talk about the 20 hours per week you spend training for the Iron Man triathlon or the summer you spent working for Greenpeace. Stay focused on presenting work as your priority and other interests as secondary.

**Sample question:** "So, what do you think about what's going on in politics right now?"

**Sample response:** "Well, I keep up with the news, and there are several issues in particular that I'm interested in and follow closely. I enjoy having political discussions with my friends and learning about their perspectives on things."

Try to avoid making any statements that reveal your political leanings. The interviewer may be testing you to see whether your views are in line with the culture of the organization. This goes for any question in which you might be forced to make a statement about your private life or about issues such as equal opportunity, women's rights, etc. And remember that questions about religious views or sexual orientation are illegal (see pages 58–59).

# the hypothetical interview

## When asked to invent the future, take time to think

Imagine an interviewer asking you these questions: "What if your boss asked you to put together a team to orient new employees? How would you select people?" Or "I'm writing a book titled, *99 Uses for Matchboxes*. Can you give me five uses for them?" These questions are asking you to imagine a future situation and how you would behave. There are several possible purposes for asking such questions.

**The job and organization need creative people.** Questions such as the matchbox one are used to see how you use your imagination. Since there are no right or wrong answers in such a situation, think creatively and have fun with the question.

**The interviewer is raising the heat.** As in the conversational interview, it is possible that the interviewer wants to know how you will respond to odd situations. It might be that the organization deals with lots of customers and that surprises occur daily with customers. The underlying question of the interview is: "Will you take a moment to think and then respond to the customer in an appropriate way?"

**The job requires a highly organized person.** Startup organizations, new departments, or areas in organizations that need to be turned around often require a person who knows how to bring step-by-step structure into an organization. Give an example of how you have brought order to a former job and you should be golden.

When asked off-the-wall, imaginary questions, take a moment to think. Breathe deeply and try to figure out how the question is relevant to the job. Once you think you know what the underlying concern is, ask the interviewer to verify this before continuing.

# Responding to a Hypothetical Question

An interviewer might ask: "What would you do if your boss went on vacation out of the country, leaving you in charge of an important project after only a month on the job, and then a serious customer problem arose that was not anticipated?"

The purpose of this question is to see how you respond to a crisis and how confident you are in taking initiative. Your goal should be to show that you understand organizational systems and hierarchies and that you are confident in making decisions.

**Your answer might go like this:**

"Well, hopefully, my boss, coworkers, and I would have a contingency plan in place for when someone is absent from the organization. I would expect that in most circumstances I would first try to reach my boss, wherever he is traveling. I might also call my boss's boss and discuss the problem with her. Before I called anyone, however, I would develop at least two solutions to deal with the problem. If I could not readily get in touch with either my boss or my boss's boss, then I would discuss the problem with a long-term employee who could probably help me understand how the organization usually handled such problems."

# the stress interview

**When the goal is to make you sweat, take a deep breath**

A few interviewers purposefully create stressful situations, believing that they are duplicating rough job conditions. If, for example, the job entails customers hanging up the phone on you, the interviewer may re-create a similar scenario to see how you will respond. Or the interviewer may adopt a challenging tone, attacking some aspect of your résumé.

What should you do? First, know your résumé very well. Don't stumble over dates and facts under probing questioning by the hiring manager or recruiter.

Second, remain calm regardless of what comes your way. If the interviewer's goal is to see how quickly he can push your hot button, then don't oblige him. If you respond angrily to an aggressive question, he is likely to respond accordingly, and then the interview will be out of control. Instead, restate the questions, taking the heat out of them. In that way, you will retain your professional composure.

Third, you should ask yourself if you really want to work for an organization that treats job candidates in such a way. These days, with the increasing focus on preserving quality of life and protecting mental health on the job, most candidates say no, which is why many organizations do not use stress interviews.

# Keeping Your Cool

The following are samples of stress interview questions and smart responses.

**Sample question:** "I see from your résumé that you graduated from Mountain State College (MSC). We've found that people from your college do not perform top-quality work for us. What makes you think that you will be better than those folks?"

**Sample response:** "Well, I obviously don't know the people you've dealt with, nor do I have knowledge of their performance here. However, I can say that I found my courses at MSC to be challenging. One of the ways MSC prepared me for your job was through leadership opportunities in student government. For example, as vice chairman of social programs I increased freshman attendance at events by 8 percent over the previous year. I can employ the same skills I used in that position to develop business opportunities for your organization."

**Sample question:** "What would you say if I told you that your interview is the worst I've ever seen?"

**Sample response** (take a deep breath and count to 3 first): "For the moment I'm going to assume that you are asking such a hostile question because you believe I will encounter similarly tough situations on the job and you want to see how I will respond. I can assure you that I remain calm under most circumstances and that allows me to problem-solve.

"For example, at my last job, when the company was in danger of closing down because a new employee had mishandled some major accounts, I stepped in to help the unhappy customers and convinced them to sign on with us again. I also retrained the new employee. In the end, I managed to bring our company out of the black within three months—*and* save everyone's jobs."

## FIRST PERSON SUCCESS STORY

### Thinking On Your Feet

I was trying for a job at a discount shoe store and almost panicked when the interviewer asked if I would be embarrassed to work for a company that sells such low-quality products. I knew the interviewer was trying to trip me up, so I replied that although the products were inexpensive, that did not mean they were cheap. Other shoe stores are overpriced, so this store offers good value for cost-conscious shoppers. I ended by saying this was the sales pitch I would use for skeptical or critical customers. This was the right answer, and I got the job.

—Krista B., Andover, Massachusetts

# the behavior-based interview

**Your past behaviors are seen as the best predictors of future ones**

Behavioral interviews use a well-defined set of questions to collect information from the candidate about how she behaved in past work situations. The assumption here is that how you performed in past situations is the best predictor of how you will behave in the future.

To develop questions for this type of interview, an employer may hire a consulting firm to interview top performers in the field for which the company is hiring. Consultants will then collect data about the competencies required to perform well in this position and use this to create specific questions that will reveal how you reacted to similar situations in the past. In essence, the organization creates a measuring tool to gauge whether you have the skills and attributes to perform well in the job.

HR personnel, managers, and executives are trained in how to ask the questions and probe for details and then to score responses of candidates. Each candidate is asked the same basic set of questions. The interviewers then discuss the highest-scoring candidates.

Research shows that using this process makes hiring decisions more objective, and the most qualified candidates are hired. So, if you are doing a fair amount of interviewing, expect to run into behavior-based interviews.

If you do encounter them, remember your success stories (see pages 16–17) and make sure to quantify the results of your past performance (for more on that, see pages 18–19). These interviews are data-driven, so the more you can quantify your past successes, the better your scores will be and the more likely you are to emerge as the candidate with the greatest future potential.

# Focusing on the Details

If a company wants to hire a sales manager, then the employer has undoubtedly identified skill sets in persuasiveness, negotiation, and teamwork for the position. The interviewer might say, "I see from your résumé that you have had considerable experience selling to large corporate buyers. Tell me about a specific sales event with a large buyer where you closed the deal. What did you do to position yourself and your firm to make the sale? How did you close the deal? What techniques did you use to demonstrate your firm's superiority to the competition?"

**Poor answer:** "Well, yes, we closed a big deal with Compaq. We went down to their headquarters and made a PowerPoint presentation. We took the guys out to dinner and talked a good deal. I don't remember any particular techniques we used to demonstrate our superiority over the competition."

**Strong answer:** "Well, yes, we closed a big deal with Compaq. We made it a point to travel to its Houston headquarters. I learn a lot about a customer's needs by speaking with the employees and observing what they do and how they operate the equipment. We asked to have lunch with Compaq's sales group before we made our PowerPoint presentation in the afternoon. I find that if I connect with people before a presentation, they tend to ask more questions. The presentation turns into a two-way conversation about our product and its strengths, which is what happened that afternoon. We positioned ourselves as a good value for Compaq's level of technological sophistication. Eventually the company wanted to order a larger volume than we expected. When I learned about the increase in the order, I immediately called my EVP to get authorization to sell at a lower price. I also talked with our manufacturing guys to see if they could speed up delivery of the product. Of course, I stayed on top of those manufacturing folks until Compaq received its order."

# the case question interview

**Before firms hire you for your mind, they *test* it**

Organizations that buy brainpower, such as business or management consulting firms, often use case questions as their preferred style of interviewing. Case interviewers ask you to solve problematic situations. In some cases, they'll ask you to talk out the solution; in other cases, they may want you to write it out.

The purpose of the case interview is to observe how you think and how you handle complex problems. Since many people find case question interviews stressful, interviewers are also watching to see how you respond to a tough situation. They want to hire smart, confident people who can think on their feet.

Some consulting firms have added interesting twists to the case question interviewing process. Candidates arrive for an interview and are handed a case; 30 to 45 minutes later they are expected to present a case analysis, as if they were in a business school classroom. Other consulting firms bring in three or four candidates and give them the same case to read. After a specified time, all the candidates gather in a room and are told they must make a presentation in an hour. Interviewers sit in the room and watch how candidates interact, noting who leads, who is passive, who adds good ideas, and who is comfortable making presentations. A well-thought-out scoring system identifies the strongest candidates. Those folks are asked to return for the next round of interviews.

If you are interviewing with a consulting firm, you'll need to do your homework on case questions in order to excel.

Some sample case interview questions:

■ How many gas stations are there in Boston?

■ Given the recent corporate scandals, what changes in corporate governance would you recommend to boards of directors?

# Thinking Outside the Box

If you are trying to get hired at a consulting firm, then you need to be prepared for the case question interview. Follow the steps listed below.

**1.** Read books and visit Web sites to learn more about the case interview. *The Vault Guide to the Case Interview* (see "Now where do I go?" on page 85) is an excellent resource.

**2.** Learn about the different types of case questions and the skills that each question assesses. *The Vault Guide* argues that there are eight types of case questions:

- falling profits
- new product introduction
- entering a new market
- entering a new geographic market
- site selection
- mergers and acquisitions
- competitive response
- changes in government/regulatory environment

**3.** Practice, practice, practice. Sit down with a knowledgeable person and have her throw different types of cases at you so that you can practice different responses. If you don't know anyone who can help you, find a coach through your college's career services office or at Vault's Live Case Interview Prep (**http://consulting.vault.com**).

# now what do I do?

## Answers to common questions

### In my last job interview, I responded to the interviewer's question and then he was silent. What was going on?

There are a couple of possible explanations for the interviewer's behavior. He might have been thinking and was not ready to talk when you stopped. Another possibility is that he remained silent until you started talking again as a tactic to push you to expand your answer. Such a tactic reminds the interviewee who is in control. Again, you may want to ask yourself if this is the kind of person and organization that you want to work for.

### I interviewed for a position at a small firm that stated in its ad that all applicants must speak Spanish. My first interviewer asked all her questions in Spanish, but the second interviewer didn't use Spanish at all. What was this all about?

Different interviewers in organizations frequently hold different ideas about the ideal candidate. Your first interviewer must feel that the ability to communicate in Spanish is critical to job success. The second interviewer either learned about your abilities from interviewer number one or sees Spanish fluency as less important than the first person. The important thing to remember is that all job-relevant skills listed on your résumé are fair game in an interview.

### I applied for a teaching job and was one of two finalists selected to return and make an hour-long presentation. Are there limits to what an interviewer can ask someone to do to get a job?

Since the job requires you to work with and present materials to kids everyday, the employer's request was appropriate. An hour-long presentation is reasonable, while an eight-hour one is not. It is common practice, in fact, to ask job applicants to give a sample performance to interviewers, in keeping with what the job requires. This is particularly true for jobs, such as sales representatives, in which one must make presentations to groups. In your particular situation, it would also be okay for the principal to explain that the school is short a teacher and ask if you would like to substitute teach for a day. If this were to happen, you want to ask immediately about pay and to keep in mind that your every move would be judged.

## Halfway through a job interview, I'm realizing that I wouldn't be challenged by the work and I'm not interested in the job. What should I do?

If you feel as if you will not be challenged by a position, there is a good chance that your interviewer will have a similar assessment of your abilities. No one wants to hire a person who will be bored. Bored employees often leave jobs or perform poorly.

Your best option in this situation is to be honest. If you are speaking with the hiring manager or a human resources person, you should tactfully state that you believe the work will be too similar to jobs you have already had. Inquire how much flexibility there is in restructuring the position to better suit your talents. Do this only if you are very interested in the organization. This tactic will most likely work if the organization is growing and hiring several people and if you have specific skills that the organization needs. Another possible outcome of an honest assessment of your skills and the needs of the organization is that at some point you will be asked to interview for a job there that matches your talents.

# now where do I go?

**WEB SITES**

CampusAccess.com, "The Case Interview"
**www.campusaccess.com/campus_web/career/ c4job_inca.htm**

MIT Careers Handbook
**http://web.mit.edu/career/www/handbook/ caseinterview.html**

**BOOKS**

**Case in Point: Complete Case Interview Preparation**
by Marc P. Cosentino

**Vault Guide to the Case Interview**
by Mark Asher, Eric Chung, and the staff of Vault

# managing tough interviewing situations

# added interview challenges

## Warning: more interview bumps ahead

As if facing a grueling stress interview wasn't tough enough, you may have to face other interview challenges that can send you into a tailspin. These added challenges may be related to something in your résumé that catches the interviewer's eye or that pops up later as the interviewer learns more about your background. Typical alarm bells for interviewers include:

**Career changes.** Interviewers may have a knee-jerk reaction and want to ask, "What do you mean you want to move from teaching into corporate marketing—you don't have any experience! And how do you know you'll even like this new career?" You'll have to

show that you have the skills required, that you know people in the industry, and that you know the jargon of the field. To an outsider looking in, you also have to sound as if you "belong."

**Gaps in work history.** If you have gone 6 to 12 months between jobs, interviewers are going to ask, "So what were you doing with your time? Why couldn't you find a job?" You will probably have to address questions about your commitment and motivation and your appeal to employers.

**Any issues that could affect your work commitment.** While work/life balance is a hot topic in management, interviewers will be nervous if you have other commitments, such as caring for an elderly relative, that will mean you are not available 24/7. You'll need to show that you will be able to meet the company's needs while meeting your own.

**Reentry into the workplace after significant time off.** Hopefully, interviewers won't ask you if there were computers when you were employed last, but their concern about up-to-date skills and knowledge will need to be addressed.

# When You Don't Fit the Mold

There's a lot you can do ahead of time to prepare for an interviewer who may have questions about your candidacy.

■ Be honest with yourself about things in your work history or lifestyle that may raise eyebrows. You may believe that dropping out to travel for two years is not a big deal, but your potential employer probably won't see it that way.

■ Be forewarned. Realize hiring managers want to see a long employment history with a linear progression in a single career. If you don't have one, plan how you are going to handle this in advance.

■ Be confident. Don't think changing careers or reentering the workforce is impossible. Hard, yes. Impossible, no. If you are going to convince the interviewer that you can do it, then you have to be thoroughly convinced of it too!

■ Be yourself. Don't apologize for what you've done or who you are. And don't try to hide it. Deceit shines through, and so does honesty.

■ Get support. Interviewing can be tough, and everyone should find some support system for dealing with the stress, frustration, and energy drain. That's even more true if you are facing the added challenges of explaining career changes or an inconsistent work history.

# changing careers

Convince the
interviewer you've
done your research

You've been a teacher but you've always wanted to do something in the entertainment field. You've grown up in dot-coms and now you want a less frenetic job at an insurance firm. It's not easy, but you can make the transition with diligence, hard work, research, and patience.

Since interviewers use past performance as a predictor of future performance, there is a clear bias in favor of candidates who have done the job before. That bias doesn't mean you can't change your career. What it does mean, however, is that you need to do two important things.

**Follow your passion, then back it up with sound knowledge.** Choose a career that excites you, and then balance this with thorough research (library, Internet, industry bulletins, and networking with key people) to find out about your new career. The combination of your excitement about the new field and your solid knowledge of it will shine through in your interview.

**Take incremental steps.** A common mistake is choosing a completely new career and industry and then finding yourself frustrated because you can't get an interview. It will be easier to market yourself for a new job if you choose one that's only a step removed from your current job. Rather than trying to simultaneously change both the function of your job (finance, sales, HR) and the industry you're in (telecommunications, education, manufacturing), change one, build experience, and then change the other.

For example, if you want to move from customer service in telecommunications to human resources in pharmaceuticals, your first move could be to take on a customer service function in a medical company. Once inside, you'll be in a better position to network your way into the HR department.

# Mental Preparation

Along with the practical preparation you need before landing an interview in a new field, you need to prepare yourself mentally for making the move. These tips may help.

**Don't discount your past experience: The skills you have may be just what that next career needs.**
Don't lose hope because you think you don't have any skills that will transfer into a new career. You just might be surprised. Let's say you were once a bartender, have finished law school, and are now trying to join a law firm. What two jobs could possibly be more different, right? Wrong. According to those who hire lawyers, bartending is great preparation for this field. Both jobs require connecting with people and getting them to reveal themselves, plus the ability to work in a high-pressure environment.

**Be prepared to put networking skills into overdrive.**
It may not be your favorite thing in the world to do, but networking plays a crucial role in changing careers. It may be that the only way you can land an interview is by working all your contacts—even people you've just met. This will require you to project yourself as confident and focused, which can be exhausting. Use the "one contact equals two more contacts" rule: For every one person you speak with, ask him for names of two others you might talk to.

**Be patient: It may take several steps to get to where you ultimately want to be.**
Wouldn't it be great if you could just snap your fingers and land your new dream job? Unfortunately, changing careers doesn't happen overnight. You may have to put in a few years in a related job or industry before completing the leap. But once you build some solid experience, it will be much easier to complete the career change because you'll have a much stronger résumé, one that won't send up as many red flags to potential employers. So hang in there—it may take time, but you'll get there.

# building relevant experience

After years of selling electronics to aerospace manufacturers, you've decided to follow your real passion, graphic design. You've researched the field, taken night courses at an art school, and used your contacts to land informational interviews. But you still haven't landed a job. Now what? To convince that skeptical design firm to hire you, you may have to back up and do two things.

**Identify transferable skills.** These are the skills you've learned in your previous jobs that will be of value to your next employer. Transferable skills usually revolve around:

| | |
|---|---|
| Getting the task done | Working well with people |
| Project planning | Team building |
| Project monitoring | Conflict resolution |
| Decision making | Negotiation |
| Budgeting | Relationship building |
| Risk analysis | Coaching, mentoring |
| Staffing, resourcing | Supervision |

**Build some related experience.** If you have no experience in the area of your career change, you will probably need to create some. This might mean:

■ taking an internship (paid or unpaid). For example, if you want to get into graphic design, you may have to take an internship designing ads for your local paper.

■ joining professional organizations related to your industry and/or sitting on new committees.

■ volunteering at a nonprofit organization. Need budgeting skills? Volunteer to sit on a school's finance committee. Need marketing skills? Work as a publicity volunteer for a local politician.

Because of the Fair Labor Standards Act, you may not be permitted to volunteer at a for-profit company. Since you'll have to be paid, offer to do a project at a very low wage. The company will get good output at a fraction of what a regular employee would cost, and you'll be able to build your skills—and get a foot in the door.

# A New Résumé for a New Career

Let's get back to the example of a teacher trying to transit into a job in the entertainment field. Once the teacher has gained some experience and thought about transferable skills, he will need a new résumé to emphasize what he'll bring to a new job. Rather than follow the traditional format, which lists jobs in chronological order and details accomplishments, he might try these strategies for highlighting skills instead.

**Profile or Accomplishments Section**
Summarize what you bring to the job. This can be several sentences or a bulleted list of the transferable skills you've accumulated through your experience.

## PROFILE

Results-driven professional with more than 20 years' experience meeting organizational objectives. Proven ability to:

- build solid relationships across diverse constituent groups
- absorb information quickly and act decisively
- present ideas clearly and concisely
- manage all aspects of complex projects

**Accomplishments Section**
List accomplishments that highlight what you've achieved and thereby show what you'll do for your new employer. You can do this with a list of accomplishments, followed by a History of Employment . . .

## ACCOMPLISHMENTS

■ Increased enrollment by more than 25 percent in five years by improving student retention

■ Developed a new curriculum in response to state mandates, which resulted in 95 percent of students passing the first assessment tests

## HISTORY OF EMPLOYMENT

Teacher, School Name, 1998–2003
(list responsibilities)

Teacher, School Name, 1990–1998
(list responsibilities)

. . . or by highlighting the transferable skills you developed in each job alongside the job descriptions.

## HISTORY OF EMPLOYMENT

Teacher, School Name, 1998–2003

| | |
|---|---|
| Problem Solving | Chaired committee to analyze falling enrollment, made recommendations, and implemented solutions. As a result, enrollment increased 25 percent over five years. |

# the career-change interview

**Convince interviewers you can do a job you've never done before**

After all your preparation, you've finally landed an interview for a job in your new field. Now you need to convince potential employers you can do this even though you're totally new to the field. What do you do?

**Have your success stories ready.** Identify accomplishments where you've shown initiative, tackled new challenges, learned quickly, and shown resourcefulness in the face of uncertainty. These are all transferable skills that will assure an employer that you'll be successful in a new job.

**Point out the transferable skills you've identified.** Make sure that as you describe your past positions you follow any statement of job responsibilities or activities with:

- "As a result, I learned . . ." This allows you to explicitly state the skills and knowledge you developed that are relevant to the job.

- "For you, this means . . ." This is your segue into how you can produce the benefit for this employer as you did for previous ones.

**Relate any relevant experiences or accomplishments** from past jobs to the requirements of the one at hand. "I taught graphic design to all my students and got them up to speed on Photoshop, which we used to produce . . ."

**Be ready to negotiate on salary.** Don't be surprised if the salary of your new job is less than the one at the job you are leaving. Remember that your current salary reflects the expertise and skills you've built over time. Now you are entering a new career, maybe in an entry-level position, so you'll need to climb that salary ladder again.

# ASK THE EXPERTS

### I'm trying to enter a new field. What should I know about this industry before I go in for an interview?

An interviewer will probably ask you why you are interested in this industry, and this is where you can show how much you know and convey your excitement about it. Before the interview, talk to people in the industry, read trade and professional journals, and visit Web sites of major companies and professional organizations.

You should be able to talk about critical incidents in the past five years that have affected the industry or profession. You should also know about key trends in the industry and outside factors that are influencing it, such as government regulations, economic shifts, technology, and population changes.

### The interviewer asked why I'm leaving my current profession. How can I answer this?

Be careful how you answer this question. The interviewer will be listening closely to determine your honesty, to pick up on any negativity, and to see if the new job will meet your expectations. Here are some strategies for a strong answer.

■ If you are pursuing a lifelong dream, then say, "I've always wanted to work in this new field, but I needed time to prepare for the change. So, these are the things I did to get ready for this career. . . ."

■ If you are looking to escape a job with no future, then say, "My last job didn't allow me to use my strengths and make the contribution I knew I could. The strengths that I hope to use here are. . ." Talk about needing greater challenges, not about being bored.

■ If you were fired because of a conflict with the boss, say, "My boss and I respected each other, but we approached work very differently." Try not to sound as if you couldn't work well with people.

■ If you were laid off, say, "My company went through a major restructuring, and my position was downsized." Be honest—this is a common reality these days and not necessarily a reflection on you!

# inconsistent work history

**You'll need to account for every gap and job change**

If you've changed careers as frequently as the weather or have been fired or laid off, you're in good company. Recent labor statistics show that the average employee stays at one job for 3.7 years, holds nine different jobs by the age of 32, and changes careers between five and seven times.

Okay, so you're not the only one out there with a work history as tangled as a Los Angeles freeway. Nevertheless, interviewers are still going to want an explanation for every gap and turn along the way. What's the best way to approach this?

**Prepare your responses in advance** and be proactive in bringing any issues up. For example, you might say, "You may be wondering why I've had four jobs in the past six years. . . ."

**Address the interviewer's underlying concerns.** When he wants you to explain a part of your work history, ask yourself what skills or attributes he may be worried you don't have. Explain how you've developed those skills over time.

**Be brief, be honest, be positive, and move on.** Belaboring the point can make you look defensive. Keep your tone matter-of-fact. Honesty is the best policy, but you can camouflage short gaps (six months or less) by organizing your résumé by the year, rather than by the month and year, that you started and ended each job.

**Take responsibility for your history.** Don't blame gaps or quick changes on the economy, industry, company, or boss. While all of those certainly may have affected your job history, the employer doesn't want a whiner or a victim. He wants someone who takes charge of her life and will take charge of her new job.

**Find a common thread.** Examine your history and see if any themes emerge that connect the gaps and changes. Have you always taken jobs that required creativity? Use that theme to tell a story of consistency and continuity across multiple jobs or careers.

# Fielding Concerns About Your Work History

## Concern: You've been in a previous job a long time.

**Question: Why haven't you been promoted?**

- Reveal increases in responsibility not reflected in job title (and maybe not seen in salary). Make sure this is also addressed in your résumé.

- Agree that this inertia is why you are looking for a new job now.

- Explain that you'd advanced as far as possible in that company. Show the hiring manager how you will be able to adapt to a new company.

- Give examples of taking on new work and working with new people.

- Position your longevity as a commitment you can bring to this new company.

## Concern: You were fired.

**Question: What did you do to get fired?**

- If due to downsizing, put it into context, stating how many were let go.

- If it was your fault, admit you made a mistake, and share what you learned.

- If you were unable to get along with the boss or others, phrase this in a positive or neutral way as a difference in work styles. Position it as a difference of opinion, with mutual respect still intact.

- Show how work still got done.

## Concern: You've changed jobs frequently.

**Question: Are you unable to commit?**

- Explain how the jobs were project-oriented or temporary.

- Portray frequent movement as your quest for a fulfilling job.

- Show how you are proactive in managing your career progress.

**Question: How do I know you won't leave after a few weeks?**

- Explain that you are now clear (due to age, other jobs) about what you want.

- Share stories that convey your perseverance, follow-through, and commitment.

## Concern: You've been out of work a long time.

**Question: Why haven't you been able to get a job?**

- Explain how you are being more selective this time.

- Demonstrate that you are now focused and ready to go!

# explaining time off

## Focus on what you learned during a work hiatus

Outside interests and personal issues may have affected your career in several ways. The time you've taken to care for elderly parents or the jobs you've quit to travel every few years may account for some of those holes or twists in your résumé. Or per-haps, because of outside commitments, you haven't shot straight up the career ladder like others in your field.

If this describes you, you may have some explaining to do when an interviewer wants to know what you did during your time off or why you haven't been promoted in a while. The interviewer may be thinking that you're not committed to your career or don't have the drive to succeed. But there are things you can do to put the inter-viewer at ease. You can explain gaps in your résumé by:

**Showing how your career continued to grow during the hiatus.** For example, if you took time off to have children, did you con-tinue moving along in your career in some way, through education, part-time work, volunteer activities, reading, or being involved in profes-sional groups? While you were trekking in Nepal, did you expand your capacity to persevere in tough circumstances?

**Connecting your experience to this new job.** For example, you could say, "I approach my job as I do my life. If I see an oppor-tunity, I go for it. If I see a challenge, I step up to the plate."

**Assuring the interviewer that the reason is resolved.** Your children may have grown, you've finished handling your parents' estate, or the once-in-a-lifetime opportunity to be part of a presi-dential campaign is over. If the reason is ongoing, explain how you are handling it.

**Presenting the benefits of returning now.** You are returning to a job after spending time reflecting on what you really want to do, getting refreshed, gaining clarity of purpose, or resolving issues, and you are now able to focus on your job and future.

# ASK THE EXPERTS

**Last year, my husband's company transferred him to another city, and I quit my job to go with him. How can I assure a new employer that this won't happen again?**

Check into the policy regarding transfers at your husband's company; it may limit the number of times employees can be transferred. If so, make sure the interviewer knows this. Or you could say that you and your husband have decided to let your job dictate where the two of you will live for the next several years.

**I've been interviewing with a company for weeks, and just a few days ago I found out that I'm pregnant. Do I need to tell the hiring manager?**

No, but it's not as simple as that. If you disclose your condition, you are offering information an employer is not allowed to legally have or use in a hiring decision. But if you withhold it until after you get a job offer, your may lose your new employer's trust. One idea: go through the interview process, sell them on your skills, and when it's time to discuss job terms (prior to an offer), disclose your pregnancy. You've already sold them on how terrific you are, so they should be willing to create a contract that works for both of you.

# FIRST PERSON SUCCESS STORY

## Bridging the Gap

When I landed an interview for my dream job as a set production manager, I didn't know how to explain why I hadn't worked in this field for two years. I didn't want to explain that I had quit my last job because I disliked my boss and needed a break from the theater world. During the interview, I explained how I used my time off to help a friend run her pottery business, and that the experience I gained by organizing her production schedule, working with outside vendors, and hiring staff are all very useful skills for a set production manager to have. I was offered the job the following week.

—Alan W., San Francisco, California

# explaining a "step down"

**M**aybe you're trying to get out of the rat race and have a more balanced life. Maybe your last job was giving you heartburn or carpal tunnel syndrome. Or maybe you need a job you can do while you raise your children or work toward a graduate degree. Whatever the case may be, you've decided that you want a less stressful job, one with less responsibility, fewer deadlines, and shorter hours. It may even be a "step down" on the career ladder.

If the interviewer wants to know what's behind this decision, your challenge is to convince her that you need a less demanding job right now but that taking a lower-level job doesn't mean you won't work hard. You also need to allay her fears that you'll get bored and leave soon or that you'll become a clock watcher, just filling in a time sheet.

Here are some ways to convince the interviewer that you're right for the job.

**Explain how this job meets your needs.** For example, "I've always taken great pride in the contributions I've made in each of my jobs. I recognize that this job has less responsibility and power than my previous one, but that's not what I'm looking for. I've learned how to lead projects and people, but I've also learned that what I really love is research and analysis, and that's what I want to do. Your job will allow me to make a valuable contribution, be a resource to the team, and continue to expand my expertise and hidden skills."

**Explain the trade-offs.** For example, you could say, "I understand I'm moving into a more junior position compared to the job I had before, but I see this as essential. I'm entering a new industry and I have to pay my dues. I want to be successful in this industry, so I'm going to put 100 percent into this job and work my way up."

# Getting Your Work/Life Needs Met

If your concern is finding a job that will allow you to balance your work and life, you're going to have to be careful about finding out whether a new job offers that. You won't be able to come right out and ask if it's a 40-hour-per-week job or what time you can leave at the end of the day. If you do, you'll risk being seen as lazy or demanding or as having too many outside commitments that could interfere with your ability to do the job.

So how can you subtly figure out whether you'll be able to leave work by 5 P.M. to pick up your kids or head to yoga class?

■ Check out the surroundings. Do employees have family pictures on their desks? Do company bulletin boards advertise company social events or athletic leagues? Does it appear that employees can bring their personal lives to work?

■ Did your interview extend well beyond 5 P.M.? If so, were there still a lot of people in the office? Drive by the company some evening. How many lights are on, and how many cars are in the parking lot at 7 P.M. or on weekends?

■ Ask indirect questions relating to leadership, rewards, and goals that reveal how the company assesses an employee's value. For example, you might ask:

"Can you name a person you see as a leader in this company and tell me what their success is based on?" Notice whether the interviewer talks about the 80-hour work weeks this employee puts in.

"What does it take to be seen as a valued contributor here?" Pay attention to what the interviewer says about quality of output or the number of hours spent in the office.

"When are meetings generally held?" If meetings are regularly held on weekends or late at night, this job may be more demanding than you want.

■ Ask what a typical day is like in the department in terms of pace, expectations, and hours. Imbed the question about hours into other queries about the position.

# now what do I do?

## Answers to common questions

### After 30 years in the military, I am now a newly retired colonel. How do I convince an employer that I can handle a civilian job and a new career at my age?

Making the transition from a career in the military to a civilian job is a difficult one. You may face similar issues as women who have spent their lives raising a family and want to enter the workforce for the first time in decades. On the plus side, many of the skills you learned in the military (administration, leadership, procurement, transportation, accounting) are the exact same skills many businesses need. On the negative side, some employers may be hesitant to hire you because of your age or inexperience in business.

There are several things you can do to convince a reluctant employer that you are willing and able to start a new career at your age.

■ Show that you are up-to-date with the latest technologies and business methods. This may mean taking a computer course, for example, or updating that dusty accounting license you earned in 1970.

■ If you've never worked for a private firm before, you'll have to show your new employer that you understand why most organizations exist: to make money. Relate success stories about setting goals and meeting them, and wherever possible, weave in business language (see pages 52–53).

■ Go for the corporate look. Adopt the standard "work uniform" (as described on page 40). Replace eyeglass frames that are more than 10 years old with more contemporary ones. Update your hairstyle.

■ Avoid formal terms of address such as "sir" and "ma'am." Beware of phrases such as "When I was young . . ." or "Back in the old days . . ."

■ Find a support network. Each military service branch has an organization charged with providing career transition support, and there are also groups for helping older people and women enter the workplace for the first time.

### I'm trying to move from a nonprofit career into the for-profit sector, but people say that's impossible. Is it?

If you've spent the last 10 years working in education, social services, philanthropy, or the government, you'll face the same hurdles as the retired colonel: Employers will question your knowledge of revenues, profits, and the bottom line. Here are some strategies that might help.

■ Learn to speak the language of business. You have to become comfortable talking about concepts such as return on investment, capital costs, margins, and breakeven. Pick up a book on finance for beginners, or enroll in a course on finance for the nonfinancial manager at your community college.

■ Apply financial principles to your nonprofit work. Look at your successes and think about how you might measure them financially. How were you able to increase the number of people you served? How were you able to provide more service without an increase in budget? It may be hard to quantify the benefits you provided, but be creative. For example, let's say you started a free after-school program for children. To increase the number of kids you were able to help, you offered internships to local high school students, giving them the chance to gain valuable work experience. This allowed you to double your enrollment, which had the secondary benefit of allowing twice as many mothers to work full-time and earn more money to raise their families. You can also talk about any money raised through fund-raising or grant-writing activities. If you reached out to the corporate community, name those companies.

# now where do I go?

## BOOKS

**So What if I'm 50**
by Bob Weinstein

**Career Change**
by Dr. David Helfand

**Barnes & Noble Basics: Résumés and Cover Letters**
by Susan Stellin

**Managing Career Transitions**
by Kit Harrington Hayes

**Getting Interviews: For Job Hunters, Career Changing Consultants, and Freelancers**
by Kate Wendleton

## WEB SITES
### Insider information on companies:

**www.companiesonline.com**

**www.vaultreports.com**

**www.wetfeet.com**

**www.hoovers.com**

**www.ceoexpress.com**

## CONTACTS

The Retired Officers Association
201 North Washington Street
Alexandria, VA 22314

## Chapter 6

# dealing with diversity

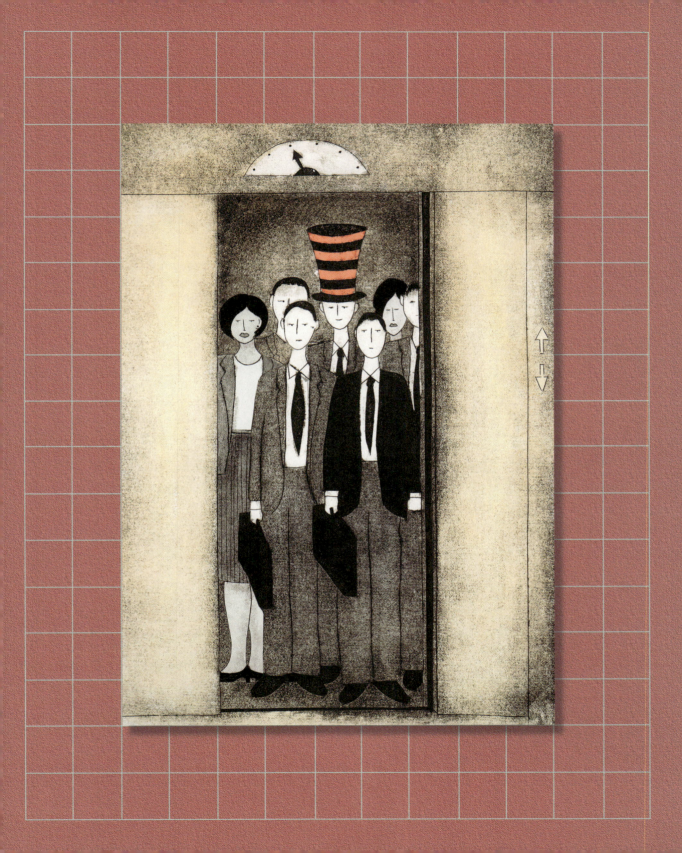

# addressing diversity

## It's likely you won't look like your interviewer

It's the morning of your interview and you're wearing your lucky interview outfit. Your shoes are polished, your answers are prepared, and you arrive on time. The receptionist greets you and leads you down the hall to the office of the hiring manager. The door swings open, and behind the desk is a man who looks like he's younger than your son.

In America's increasingly diverse workforce you are likely to encounter people from a broad range of backgrounds, and you should not be surprised if you're confronted by an interviewer who is radically different from you.

When you walk in the door, it may also turn out that you're the one who doesn't fit the mold. You may be an older worker or a very young one. You could belong to a minority group, have a physical disability such as a speech disorder, or be very overweight—and any of those things can throw an interviewer off.

As with all interview situations, however, you can prepare to tackle these potential challenges before the interview starts.

# Addressing the Issue of Fit

Remember the top three concerns of an employer: Do you have the skills? Do you have the motivation? And will you fit in? The more different you are from your employer, the greater his concern about fit will be. Here are some ways to help him see beyond your differences.

**Don't lose your cool.** Even an interviewer who is used to meeting candidates from all walks of life may be taken aback when meeting you if you're not a "typical" interviewee. Or *you* may be the one who's surprised. Whatever the case, try to respond to issues of diversity with equanimity.

**Put the interviewer at ease.** While it should be the *interviewer's* job to make you feel welcome, don't wait for him to do so. Use light humor, find common interests, and keep the conversation going.

**Take charge and talk about any differences openly and matter-of-factly.** There's a good chance an interviewer won't bring up concerns about any obvious difference due to his own discomfort or fear of legal issues. But if you don't bring it up, you may leave the interview with a potential barrier still in place. So, for example, you might say, "You may be wondering how my wheelchair impacts how I can accomplish the job. Let me give you some examples of how my boss and I were able to come up with very workable solutions in the past." This gives the employer permission to ask questions that relate to your ability to perform the job.

**Be comfortable about your differences.** The more self-confident you are, the more comfortable your interviewer will be. Don't apologize or make self-deprecating comments.

**Follow the rules of the organization.** Fitting in often means following the established rules. So, follow the interviewer's lead about language and etiquette (for more on this, see pages 50–51).

**Be open-minded.** Try to find a balance between being overly sensitive to potential discrimination and ignoring it altogether. Stay focused on what you can do to ace the interview, build credibility as a candidate, and advance your career.

# strategies for older workers

**Emphasize the positive contributions older workers can make**

Age will certainly influence what happens in your interviews, unless your interviewer is roughly equal to your age. In many cases, there's a good chance you will be much older than the person interviewing you—especially if you are meeting with a junior HR screener.

It's not uncommon for older workers to encounter subtle ageism in young interviewers. If you are an older worker, you will need to assure the interviewer you can handle the job. These myths and stereotypes include the beliefs that, as an older worker, you:

- are less able and willing to learn new skills
- have obsolete skills and knowledge
- are less healthy and so will be absent more often
- have reduced capabilities, work more slowly, and are likely to make more errors
- will be a drain on the pension plan since you will work fewer years before retiring
- are expensive both in terms of higher salary and the cost of benefits, particularly when it comes to health care

How do you counter these myths? You need to identify indirect ways to make the employer understand that, as an older worker, you:

- are more stable and less likely to job-hop
- may no longer have the family demands faced by workers with young children
- have well-developed and proven skills
- are more realistic in your expectations about work
- bring more maturity and better judgment to the job
- may have a large network of business connections
- are among a group that surveys show has lower turnover and absenteeism
- may need little or no training

During the interview, make sure to share success stories that refute negative stereotypes, and emphasize the benefits of hiring you.

# Interview Tactics to Take the Years Off

**Don't show surprise at the interviewer's age.** You may be amazed that she is young enough to be your daughter, but don't mention it!

**Don't apologize for your age.** This positions your age as a liability. It isn't.

**Don't show your own stereotypes.** Don't refer to women as "gals" or "girls" or call them "honey" or "dear." Don't refer to men as "boys" or call them "son."

**Counter the prevailing stereotypes.** Not energetic? Speak crisply and enthusiastically. Not nimble? Share examples of times you showed quick thinking. Not computer literate? Speak confidently about technology and applications. Better yet, e-mail your résumé, maintain contact by e-mail, and talk about the great things you learned about the company on its Web site.

**Talk about recent accomplishments.** Stay away from successes you achieved 20 years ago. What have you accomplished in the past year?

**Be positive and energetic.** Those are the two greatest attributes employers are looking for—and the two biggest reservations they have about older workers.

**Watch for warning signs.** "You're overqualified" or "We can't afford you" can be signs of age discrimination. If you hear this, probe this concern carefully to figure out what the real issue is.

## Getting the Interview

If you want to increase the chances of getting called in for an interview, avoid age revelations in your résumé and cover letter.

■ Don't start out your cover letter with "Over my 30 years of experience . . ."
■ You don't have to put college graduation dates on your résumé.
■ Your work history needs to go back only 10 to 15 years.
■ Any experience prior to that can be lumped into an Other Experience category that lists relevant and interesting positions without dates.

# strategies for younger workers

## It's all about building credibility

**W**hat about the flip side? You show up for an interview and you're met by a man old enough to be your grandfather. The stereotypes work both ways. Many employers feel that younger workers:

- lack the skills to produce good work
- have book smarts but no real experience
- aren't committed and will jump ship at a moment's notice
- don't know what hard work and perseverance are all about
- aren't willing to start at the bottom and pay their dues

Fight these stereotypes by finding subtle ways to remind the interviewer of the benefits of younger employees. Young workers often:

- come as a clean slate with no bad habits to break
- are easier to train
- don't suffer from "been there, done that" syndrome
- are comfortable with new technology, change, and uncertainty
- will do the less desirable tasks and work the less desirable hours

For you, the primary challenge is building credibility. Present your education as actual work experience. Talk about the skills you developed in college that would be useful in this position: meeting deadlines, working in teams, making presentations, organizing projects. Tell success stories that prove your claims and build a track record. Show respect for the interviewer's experience and a willingness to learn from him.

Describe your schoolwork positively. Chances are the entry-level jobs you are now applying for have many of the same characteristics you disliked about school: lots of routine tasks, no visibility, little power and control. Try to focus on all the skills you learned in school and how you can apply them to this new job.

If you worked while in school, make sure the interviewer knows you helped finance your education. This shows initiative, time management, responsibility, and maturity.

# ASK THE EXPERTS

## What if an interviewer asks me how I would feel about working with much older coworkers?

You basically have three ways to respond. You can:

- point out that the question is discriminatory and end the interview. Realize this means that you have likely lost any chance at this job.

- gently ask, "Can you explain how age is a factor in performing the job?"

- answer the question briefly and put a positive spin on it. "In college, I got to know many older professionals, such as professors, and developed mutually beneficial working relationships with them."

## What if I think my age is being counted against me?

If you think you're getting nowhere because of your age, say, "I'm wondering if you're concerned about my age. Let me address that for a moment. I believe my youth is an asset because . . ." Then take the assets of youthful workers, listed on the previous page, and link them to the particular attributes you bring to the position.

## Overcoming Concerns About Your Age

The Age Discrimination in Employment Act (1978) prohibits employers from discriminating on the basis of age and prevents them from asking direct questions to identify how old you are. Employers can ask if you are of a legal age to do the job, but asking "How old are you?" or "When were you born?" is not okay. They can, however, ask you to provide proof of your age once hired if age is a "bona fide occupational qualification," such as being over the minimum age required to serve alcohol or operate machinery.

# dealing with disability

## The critical questions should be the same

If you are a disabled job candidate, you will probably need to spend some time persuading an interviewer that you can do the job. First of all, don't surprise your interviewer with your disability. The ADA (Americans with Disabilities Act) leaves it up to you to request any special accommodations for an interview. This can be a subtle way of letting the employer know about your disability. You do run the risk of suddenly being told the job is already filled, but do you want to waste your time with that kind of an organization anyway?

Be sure to ask ahead of time what will be included in the interview. If there's a typing test and you need your own keyboard, bring it. Bringing your own adaptive technologies is a great way of demonstrating how you can be resourceful.

While it is the interviewer's job to put you at ease, you may have to take control of the situation and help the interviewer feel comfortable. The more easygoing and friendly you are, the better your chances. It's normal for the interviewer to feel awkward and cautious about saying the wrong thing. By making the interviewer feel comfortable, you are answering one of the key questions of any employer: Do I want to work with this person? Be forthright, and address disability right away; otherwise, it will be the elephant in the middle of the room that no one wants to talk about. Certainly you don't want to spend the entire time talking about your disability, but you do want to answer any questions that may be lingering in the mind of the interviewer.

Assure the interviewer you can do the job by telling success stories illustrating your skills (see pages 16–17). Give references who can attest to your abilities.

Be honest about the accommodations you'll need to perform the job and briefly share what has worked well in the past. Many employers may fear that it will cost too much to accommodate your needs. Research has found the opposite is true: 31 percent of accommodations cost nothing, and 51 percent cost under $500. Cite statistics and examples to overcome objections about the cost of accommodating you.

## Good Companies

Disabled job seekers should look into disability-friendly firms. According to *WE* magazine, a lifestyle publication for people with disabilities, these firms include IBM, Marriott, AT&T, Hertz, Nabisco, Ford, and Northwest Airlines. Visit *WE* magazine's Web site (**www.wemagazine.com**) to learn more.

# Dealing with Disability Concerns

**Know what the employers can and cannot ask.** The ADA prohibits employers from asking questions about the existence, nature, or severity of a disability until after a conditional job offer has been made. The legality of a question hinges upon whether it is job related.

**These questions are legal:**

■ Can you perform the essential functions of this job, with or without reasonable accommodation?
■ Can you demonstrate these functions?
■ Can you stand on your feet for six hours, if that is part of the job?
■ Will you agree to take a medical exam once a job offer has been extended?

**These questions aren't legal:**

■ How many days were you out sick last year?
■ Have you ever filed for workers' compensation?
■ How is your health?
■ How did you develop this disability?

Reveal an active, interesting life. There's a natural curiosity about the world of the disabled. Though this curiosity may feel invasive and frustrating to you, the fuller a picture you can paint of who you are (complete with hobbies, sports, and outdoor activities), the easier it will be for the interviewer to picture working alongside you.

# gendered expectations

**Understanding the rules will help you stay on top of the interview**

**M**en and women often follow different rules regarding what they believe is appropriate behavior during an interview. For instance, when an interviewer asks "Can you do the job?" a male candidate might say "yes" and a female candidate might say "I'll try." American culture teaches men to talk about outcomes, speak directly, exaggerate, and take sole credit for their accomplishments. Women are taught to talk about relationships, speak indirectly, understate their accomplishments, and share credit for them with others. These differing cultural expectations can create havoc in an interview situation, leading to confusion, misinterpretation, and, at worst, no job offer.

So how can you handle these gendered expectations? Try to speak the language of your interviewers. Listen to their questions to determine what's important to them. Do they keep asking about

results? If so, talk about results, not relationships. Do they use exaggerated language ("always," "best," "worst")? If so, describe your work as "outstanding," not "pretty good."

Watch their reactions. Are they shying away from you? If so, tone down the volume. Are they unimpressed with your success story (see pages 16–17) about team building? If so, tell a story about getting the task done on your own against all odds.

# ASK THE EXPERTS

### What should I do if an interviewer asks me about my plans for marriage and children?

Before reacting, try to determine what the underlying issue might be. You could ask, "Can you explain how that applies to this position?" or answer, "If you're concerned about my willingness to do what it takes to get the job done, let me give you an example of my commitment," and follow with a success story (see pages 16–17).

### An HR manager I was meeting with said, "Hey, you've got great legs. Are you a dancer?" What was I supposed to do?

If a question makes you uncomfortable, the interviewer may be purposely trying to throw you off balance, or he may be oblivious to his behavior. If you think it was innocent, sidestep it by saying, "I don't see how that question is relevant to the job," and proceed with the interview. If you think it was intentional sexual harassment, put up a fire wall. You could say, "Excuse me, but I'm not comfortable with how this interview is proceeding. Could you please stop this line of questioning?" If he continues, say, "I can see this interview is going nowhere," and leave. Then tell the person who is organizing the recruitment process what happened. Understand that if you walk out of an interview, you're not going to get that job. But then, do you really want to work in such an environment?

### I'm just starting my job search. How can I find out which companies are rated the best for female employees?

Many sources put out lists each year of the top 25 companies for women. These lists are based on criteria such as hiring, promotion, retention of women, and benefits such as child care and maternity leave. You can find these lists in *Fortune* and *Working Woman* magazines. For a collection of facts about working women and companies, check out **www.ewowfacts.com/index.html**.

# the cross-cultural divide

**Your interviewer may be following rules from a different culture**

Brag about your accomplishments! Focus on your impact on business! Make direct eye contact! Don't talk about your family and your outside interests! All good advice to follow when interviewing. Right? Well, maybe . . . and maybe not.

These rules are being challenged by the increasingly diverse cultural and ethnic groups in the United States. You've read the statistics, so recognize that when you walk in for an interview, there's a good chance your interviewer will have a different cultural origin than you. And she may have different expectations about how you should conduct and market yourself; that's because every culture has its own rules for interviews. In Europe, for example, you would be asked about your family, your husband, and your children (or plans for them). In the United States, that conversation is illegal.

An interviewer from a different cultural background may start out following American interviewing rules but slip into the rules of her own culture. So, during the interview you'll need to determine which rules she is following. You can do this by being aware of how the interviewer greets and addresses you, paying attention to the kinds of questions she asks, and watching her body language. The more you mirror your interviewer's behavior, the more likely she is to view you in a positive light. (For more on this, see pages 54–55.)

The same thing goes if your own cultural background is not American. If you follow interview rules from your own culture, you may be viewed poorly by the interviewer. Do your best to mold your tactics to the interviewer's so that you come across as a good fit. And before you go into the interview, make sure to practice your responses to typical questions with an experienced colleague or friend.

# How Can You Bridge the Cultural Divide?

Use these strategies to combat cultural stereotypes during an interview.

**Help interviewers pronounce your name.** If you have a name that is hard for people to pronounce, you may want to include a guide for pronouncing it or an English equivalent in parentheses on your résumé. Recruiters have been known to screen out résumés with unfamiliar names simply to save themselves the embarrassment of mispronouncing names when they call to set up interviews. When meeting interviewers, always clearly pronounce your name for them.

**Don't let interviewers pigeonhole you.** If the HR screener wants to slot you into a certain job because "your people are good at that," gently but firmly insist on applying for the job you want. Clearly spell out the education, experience, and skills that qualify you.

**Assure interviewers that you will fit in.** You can do this by following their rules for behavior and dress. That means dressing in standard corporate attire, keeping hair and jewelry simple, and using standard English.

## FIRST PERSON SUCCESS STORY

### When in Rome . . .

I applied for a job at the U.S. headquarters of a Japanese company, and I knew that I was going to be interviewed by the Japanese V.P. So I did a little research on Japanese etiquette—and it's a good thing I did! When I showed up for the lunchtime interview, I knew to remove my shoes and not to refuse the rice whiskey that was poured for me. I was careful to address my host formally, keep the jokes to a minimum, and to let him set the pace for the meal. Also, I knew not to be too aggressive in making eye contact and not to brag about my accomplishments. I later heard that he disliked the casual, chummy attitude of the other candidates, and after a few more interviews, I was the one who got the job.

—Randall P., Atlanta, Georgia

# dealing with discrimination

**Be careful of crying wolf when you think you're facing discrimination**

When you don't get that job offer, it's easy to blame the rejection on discrimination, particularly if you are a member of a group that is protected from discrimination under state and federal laws. These laws prohibit hiring decisions from being affected by the candidate's mental or physical disability, national origin, ancestry, sex, age, pregnancy, race, or religious beliefs.

But before you claim discrimination and file a suit, take a hard, thoughtful look at the entire interview process.

**Ask yourself some tough questions.** What did the job require that you may not have had? Is there anything else you could have done better to sell yourself?

**Ask the employer for insight.** For example, you can ask the hiring manager why you didn't get the job. While many employers won't give you anything more than the standard "We hired the best candidate," some will give you valuable feedback on ways you can improve your candidacy next time around.

**Ask a third party.** Describe what happened in the interview to someone who will be objective and ruthlessly frank. What is this person's view of the situation?

If, after careful reflection, you decide that there is discrimination at play here, you may decide to go forward. You'll need to do two things.

**Determine that you have a case.** Legal action may be warranted if you were asked illegal questions or the interviewer's behavior was threatening in some way. (If the interviewer was simply rude or inept, you don't have a case.) Having documentation, such as an e-mail or letter, strengthens your case.

**File a claim.** If you want to proceed, you'll need to file a complaint with the Equal Employment Opportunity Commission (EEOC), which has offices in all major cities. Find out more at **www.eeoc.gov**.

# Job-Related Legislation

An employer does not have to give you a job because you belong to a protected group. You're protected, not entitled, by the federal laws listed below. But check your specific state and city laws, because they supersede these federal laws. For example, in some states sexual orientation and obesity are protected by laws. Here's a rundown of federal legislation that may apply to you.

**The Americans with Disabilities Act (1990)**
Prohibits discrimination based on mental or physical disability, as long as those disabilities don't prevent you from doing the job. The act also requires the employer to provide reasonable accommodations, such as adaptive equipment, to enable you to perform critical job tasks.

**The Immigration Reform and Control Act (1986)**
Prohibits the employment of illegal aliens but also protects you against discrimination based on national origin or citizenship status.

**The Age Discrimination in Employment Act (1978)**
Prohibits discrimination against applicants age 40 or older.

**The Pregnancy Discrimination Act (1978)**
Prohibits discrimination against pregnant women in the hiring process and during their employment. This also applies to women with pregnancy-related medical conditions.

**The Civil Rights Act (1964)**
Prohibits employment discrimination based on race, sex, national origin, ancestry, or religious beliefs.

# now what do I do?
## Answers to common questions

### I have a birthmark on my face that seems to totally distract interviewers. How do I get them to pay attention to what I'm saying, not to what I look like?

Many physical attributes can distract your interviewer: weight, birthmarks, birth defects, or even blushing. A well-trained interviewer will move quickly past how you look, but less experienced ones may not. A powerful strategy is to mention the physical attribute up front and then segue into your skills and successes. Name it, explain it, assure interviewers that it has no impact on your ability to work, and move on. Be confident and matter-of-fact. If you don't make it an issue, neither will they.

### During an interview, I was asked some invasive questions about my religion. I just found out I didn't get the job. Do I have a discrimination case?

Carefully consider these factors before deciding to go forward with litigation.

**Clarify your motivations.** Do you really want to shed light on an illegal practice? Or are you looking for revenge or a way of shifting the blame away from yourself for not getting the job?

**Realize the costs involved.** You are signing yourself up for a long, expensive, frustrating process. There are financial fees, but also personal costs. As your time and energy get consumed by the case, your ability to continue a job search may be severely limited.

**Consider the likely outcomes.** Because of how difficult it is to prove discrimination, in most cases the company wins. Even if you do win, you will probably get only a job offer—and do you really want to work there after that? You certainly won't get rich. The most you'll get is back pay from the time you should have started working for the company. But don't get excited: The judge will subtract all the money you have been earning from whatever job you have been working at or, if you've remained unemployed, the money you should have been earning over the one to two years it took to get the case to court. Next come the lawyers' fees. . . . You get the picture.

You can also call your local bar association to find a lawyer and get advice on whether to proceed or not. Some law schools have clinics where students offer free advice.

# now where do I go?

## OLDER EMPLOYEES

The American Association of Retired Persons (AARP)
**www.aarp.org**
800-424-3410

Forty Plus Club
West Coast: 415-430-2400
East Coast: 212-233-6086

## EMPLOYEES WITH DISABILITIES

Americans with Disabilities Act Information Line
800-514-0301

Department of Justice's ADA Web Page
**www.usdot.gov/crt/ada/adahom1.htm**

Job Accommodation Network
**www.jan.wvu.edu**
800-526-7234

African Americans with Disabilities, Inc.
P.O. Box 86291
Pittsburgh, PA 15221
413-392-4407

## SEXUAL DYNAMICS

**Talking from 9 to 5**
by Deborah Tannen

**You Just Don't Understand**
by Deborah Tannen

**Disappearing Acts**
by Joyce Fletcher

**Our Separate Ways: Black and White Women and the Struggle for Professional Identity**
by Ella L.J. Edmondson Bell and Stella M. Nkomo

**www.ewowfacts.com/index.html**
A collection of facts about working women and companies.

## CULTURAL DIFFERENCES

**Dos and Taboos Around the World**
by R.E. Axtell

**Breaking Through: The Making of Minority Executives in Corporate America**
by David Thomas

**Cross-Cultural Dialogues**
by Craig Storti

**Black Enterprise Magazine**
**www.blackenterprise.com**
List of the best companies for minorities.

## EMPLOYMENT LAW

**www.findlaw.com**
Legal information on the Web.

**www.usdot.gov/crt/ada/adahom1.htm**
Information about the ADA from the Department of Justice.

**http://supct.law.cornell.edu/supct**
Latest Supreme Court rulings, including those related to harassment.

## WEB SITES

**www.CareerJournal.com**
*The Wall Street Journal*'s career column, with great articles on all aspects of job hunting and interviewing.

**www.wetfeet.com**
Great Web site with books (electronic or printed) such as *Job Search 101: Communicating Effectively*, 2003 edition, and *Job Search 101: Networking, Interviewing, and Getting the Offer*, 2002 edition.
The Web site also has many useful articles, such as "How to Handle Your First Round Interviews" and "How to Conquer Pre-Interview Jitters."

**Chapter 7**

# the second interview

# second round and beyond

**Prepare yourself
for the next steps**

You've survived the curveballs and other surprises of a first interview, and you've been called in for the second round. Before you start getting anxious, pat yourself on the back. When you get a call back, it means the screeners have determined you have the technical skills for the job. Now it's time to meet the people who will be assessing whether you will actually be right for the job, such as:

**The hiring manager.** You will probably interview with this person several times. In many ways, she acts as another screener: If she likes you, she'll send you to interview with others in the organization. Afterward, you'll meet with her again to review the feedback she's received from others and ideally to start negotiations.

**The influencers.** In many organizations, the boss won't make the hiring decision alone, but will listen to the views of up to a dozen other people who have spoken with you. While they may not be able to give the final yes, a strong objection from any one of them could mean that the hiring manager will say no. Who are they?

- Coworkers from your future department
- Peers in other divisions with whom you will collaborate
- Technical experts from across the company
- The hiring manager's manager
- Customers or vendors with whom you will interact

## FIRST PERSON SUCCESS STORY

### The Big Picture

I was so nervous about the second interview that I couldn't sleep. Finally, to get myself to relax I decided to read all the industry trade journals I hadn't had time to look at. When it came time for the second interview, I realized that I didn't have to go over my technical skills again. Now the interviewers wanted to know how I saw the big picture. Thanks to my midnight readings, I could show them that I was up-to-date with the industry issues they were facing. That really made me stand out from other, not-as-well-prepared candidates. A week later, I was called back and offered the job.

—Candace R., Boulder, Colorado

# Interview with Your Future Boss

Finally, you've passed all the screening interviews and you are face-to-face with the decision maker—your future boss. This is the person for whom you will be working, the person who will decide whether you get the job or not. The rules to this interview are slightly different than with a screener. When interviewing with a prospective boss:

**1.** Showcase your professional skills. He doesn't want to hear the details of your past jobs, but wants to know what you've cumulatively learned over your many jobs. These larger skills include building relationships, making decisions, resolving conflict, working collaboratively, and managing projects.

**2.** Show how you connect with people by telling success stories (see pages 16–17) that highlight your people skills. Even more importantly, try to connect with him. Ask him questions, such as:

- As a manager, how do you motivate your employees to give their all?

- In your opinion, which is better: putting off a deadline a bit to preserve morale, or pulling an 80-hour workweek to get the job done?

- What kinds of traits and behaviors make people successful around here?

**3.** Show off the information you've learned about the company, and ask questions that reveal your familiarity with the industry, such as:

- How are current business events (name them) affecting your company?

- If (a particular) regulation is passed, how will that affect your company's ability to market your product?

**4.** Demonstrate the kind of behavior the boss would want from a future employee: Be respectful and polite, and demonstrate good listening and communication skills.

# strategic interviewing

**To demonstrate your value, solve the company's problems**

Emphasizing your professional skills, working style, and industry knowledge is excellent. But what else can you do in the second interview to stand out? One strategy is to approach the company like a consultant—someone who is hired to analyze a particular problem a company is having and find ways to fix it.

Rather than viewing yourself as just another candidate for the job, take an active interest in the challenges the company is facing and imagine that you are the consultant brought in to tackle these issues. Ask questions to pinpoint critical problems, find out what the optimal situation would look like, and then offer some initial solutions. You can also share what you have done in similar situations in the past.

Whatever you do, though, be careful about your tone. You don't want to sound condescending or disparaging—aim instead for a positive and helpful tone. And avoid using trigger words like "problems" or "failures." Instead, ask:

- What **challenges** is the department facing?

- What **opportunities** aren't being capitalized on?

- What **changes** would you like to see around here?

The basic rule of thumb is that the higher up in the organization you interview, the broader and more strategic you—and your questions—need to become.

# Taking a Consultant's Approach

Before you go in for your second interview, take a look at these questions and think about how you can work some of them in. Once you cover the challenges a company is facing, approach them as a consultant would and make specific suggestions, drawing on your knowledge of the company. Sure, you're giving free advice—but the company might just hire you to put your strategies into action.

**Resources:** How are resources allocated to various departments, and are there any issues surrounding this?

**Financial goals:** What are some of the major challenges this department faces in reaching its financial goals?

**Production goals:** How effective is the company in reaching its production goals?

**Customers:** How does the company measure a customer's satisfaction? What would customers say you need to improve on?

**Reputation within the company:** What would another department say about this department? Why? What would you like them to say?

**Competition:** How does the company handle competition by other firms? Where is it vulnerable?

**The future:** What is the long-term forecast for the company and the market? What opportunities are expected on the horizon? What threats?

# the panel interview

**Get a grip on what can be a chaotic process**

Surprise! You show up for your second interview . . . and you find yourself face-to-face with not one, not two, but four, five, or even more people from the company who are ready to interview you. While this can be a challenge, you can handle it. All your prospective boss is trying to do is get as much information as possible about you, and a panel interview is often the most expedient way to do it.

Panel interviews are efficient for the employer, but they can be very hard on the candidate, especially if each member asks totally unrelated questions or competes with other members for airtime, interrupting your response to one question with a question of his own.

Whether you are meeting with interviewers individually, in pairs, or as a group, your goal is to make a connection with each person. Each positive connection means one more vote in your favor.

The challenge is that each person in a panel interview brings his own unique expectations about what your future job requires and what the chosen candidate should look like. Your task is to convince each person that you can meet those expectations. To do that, try to make a connection with each one when you answer his question. Look him in the eye and try to address him by name. Yes, there's a chance you'll get questions from one of the members who finds your qualifications lacking and homes in on your weaknesses. Gently steer the topic back to the skills you have and how well they relate to the job at hand. Just remember to stay calm and focus on one person at a time, and you'll succeed!

# Acing a Panel Interview

**Greet everyone individually if possible.** Greet them, shake hands, introduce yourself, and get their names (and their business cards—you can place them on the table in front of you to remind you of their names and positions at the table).

**Include everyone in your response.** While only one person asked the question, everyone is listening, so make eye contact with everyone as you respond.

**Use their names whenever possible.** It's difficult to make a connection with lots of people at once, but using their individual names helps. Refer back to Tom's question. Or ask Judy whether you addressed her concern sufficiently.

**Assume everyone is important.** Don't make assumptions about who is the decision maker in the room and who isn't. That quiet wallflower in the back may actually be the boss's boss. Or that person who doesn't ask any questions and avoids eye contact may have a lot of influence on the hiring decision.

**Be succinct.** Your goal (and theirs) is to answer as many questions as possible. It's not to answer a few questions to the fullest degree. Panel members will be unhappy if your rambling responses mean they don't have time to ask their own questions.

**Ask them questions.** Panels are a great opportunity to ask questions about the organization's culture, mission, challenges, threats, and opportunities. And there's sure to be disagreement among the members, which will add to the chaos but also to your knowledge of the company!

**Thank them.** Follow up with a thank-you note to every member of the panel. This is another good reason to get business cards up front! Each note should be unique because the interviewers may compare them.

# meeting with coworkers

**Connect with them and they'll recommend you to the boss**

Hiring managers often ask your potential coworkers to interview you. Coworkers often know best what the job demands and can ask very insightful questions. Unfortunately, many coworkers are not very good at interviewing, and some may be nervous about the effect you may have on their work life should you be hired. Some may:

- not be trained in interviewing skills

- see it as an interruption to getting their "real" job done

- have an assessment form to complete regarding your qualifications and resent this extra work

- think "Why bother? The decision won't be made by me anyway."

## With all that potentially going on, what can you do to make these interviews a success?

**1. Make the process easy for coworkers and try to create rapport.**

- Introduce yourself and mention the skills you have to offer.

- Fill in awkward pauses by asking them some of your prepared questions or offering another success story.

- Take cues regarding when the interview should conclude. Has it been around 30 minutes? Have you covered everything you'd like? If so, then subtly begin to close the interview.

**2. Make the process fun for them. Not only does this help make the situation less awkward, but it shows them that you would be enjoyable to work with.**

- Ask them questions about their jobs and their careers.

- Share humorous stories about your own work experience.

- Ask questions about their lives. What do they do outside of work? Do employees go on a lot of social outings together?

- Don't ask any gossipy questions or make anything except positive remarks about the other employees you have met.

# SK THE EXPERTS

### When I talk to potential coworkers, what's the best way to portray myself? Do I want to seem like an independent go-getter or just "one of the gang"?

Try to strike a balance. You want to assure your coworkers that you can do the job, because coworkers want you to make their lives easier. So tell them success stories that demonstrate your ability to learn quickly and highlight your self-reliance in dealing with new situations.

And reassure them that you'll do your share of the work. A coworker certainly doesn't want to work with a person who will add to his everyday work pressure. Emphasize your teamwork skills and your willingness to pitch in on projects.

### I'm sensing that a company I'm interviewing with has some internal problems. When I meet with coworkers, is it okay to ask for their insider information?

Yes, just be careful about suggesting what kind of problem you're sensing—it could very well be that your coworkers are somehow responsible. You can, however, couch your concerns in general questions about the company, such as:

What do you like/dislike about working here?
What is the performance review process like here?
Does this place really have an open-door policy?

Whatever you do, don't talk about change. You are entering their world. They will expect you to follow their ways of doing things, at least until you've earned the right to criticize and initiate changes that you would make.

# meeting the big boss

**As you go up the chain of command, remember who you're talking to**

For some jobs, you not only have to meet with your future boss and coworkers, but you must also get the nod of approval from your boss's boss. This person could be the head of the division or department or even the president of the company. What you need to know is that, just as the screener's job was to confirm that you had the right technical skills, the senior boss's job is to see that you understand the bigger picture. He or she wants to know:

■ Do you understand how your role influences the larger organization, its other parts, and its ability to reach its goals?

■ Do you see room in the organization for you to work toward your career aspirations?

■ Are you flexible enough to be called upon to apply your skills to problems wherever they arise in the organization?

■ Are you going to stay long enough to provide a worthwhile return on the company's investment in you?

In return, you need to find out from the senior boss:

■ What is the primary challenge facing the company today? How is it affecting operations, morale, and profitability? What are the current plans to address that problem?

■ What are the risks or opportunities influencing this department's ability to reach its goals? What are the key metrics for measuring its success?

■ What hurdles do you expect a new employee to face in this particular job? What needs to be tackled first?

■ What kinds of things make a person successful around here?

# Common Mistakes

You may have impressed the hiring manager, and everyone in the office would love to work with you, but you haven't gotten the job offer yet. The boss's boss can still give you a thumbs-down. Here are some reasons this might happen.

**Mistake #1: You portray yourself as fitting in so well that it seems you won't add anything new to the organization.**

**Example:** All of your coworkers think you're well qualified for the job: You have the degree and the solid experience the job requires. They all agree you'd be great to work with. The senior boss, however, is looking for someone to fill in the gaps and bring a fresh approach to problems. Having a team with diverse experience is what matters most to him, so he vetoes your candidacy.

**Mistake #2: You become too casual too soon in the process.**

**Example:** You are so convinced you have the job that when you meet the boss, you start talking to him as if the two of you were old colleagues. Instead of being professional and selling yourself, you slouch in the chair and tell jokes. This makes the boss think you have no idea how to act around the senior managers you'd be working with, so he gives your candidacy a pass.

**Mistake #3: You come across as stiff and set in your ways for a job that requires a flexible, creative approach.**

**Example:** When interviewing with the senior boss for a creative position, you rely so heavily on your portfolio that you are unable to answer spontaneous questions about what you would bring to the organization. Due to your inability to deviate from the script, the boss decides you don't possess the ability to think outside the box, something highly important for this position, and he hires someone else.

# making presentations

**You've told them you're good at presenting— now you have to "walk the talk"**

If public speaking and making presentations are job requirements, don't be surprised if you are asked to give a presentation as part of the interview process. Typically, you will be given a topic to present and a few days to prepare it. Your future boss is not asking you to make a presentation just to torture you. He wants to test your skills and knowledge, specifically:

■ your public speaking skills. Many jobs involve making presentations, whether internally to other departments or externally to vendors, clients, investors, or the public.

■ the image that you portray, because that image will be linked to the organization whenever and wherever you present.

■ your thinking and writing abilities. Good presentations follow a logical order of thought. Your boss will want to see how well you structure your presentation.

Employers who give you no advance notice about making a presentation (and give you only 15 to 30 minutes to prepare) may also be trying to see how well you perform under pressure and how well you speak extemporaneously.

## FIRST PERSON SUCCESS STORY

### Hands-down winner

I was given two days to prepare a 15-minute PowerPoint presentation, and because I was changing careers, the presentation was on a medical subject I knew absolutely nothing about. And it was going to be in front of a panel of scientists. I researched night and day on the Web and then practiced till I was blue in the face. And it was worth it—my presentation went great! But what really impressed them were my handouts. None of the other candidates had any. Not only did I have hard copies of my PowerPoint slides, but I also included relevant articles from medical journals, product marketing literature from the company's competitors, and lists of resources from professional associations. As I left the room I heard one scientist say, "She's got the job."

—Janet B., St. Paul, Minnesota

# Step by Step
# to an Unforgettable Presentation

**1.** Find out what is expected in terms of:

**Time:** How long should it be? Usually you are given 5 to 15 minutes to present.

**Q&A:** If there is a Q&A period, how much time is allotted for it?

**Topic:** Is there a specific topic the employer wants you to address, or is the topic up to you?

**Context:** Employers will often supply you with an imaginary context for your presentation—for example, a speech aimed at a major client or new employees.

**Visual aids:** What is expected and what technology/equipment is available?

**Hard copies:** Are you expected to provide printouts of your visuals and/or script? If so, find out how many copies you will need to make.

**Facilities:** Where will it take place? How will the room be set up? Will you have to use a microphone?

**2.** Find out what the organization's norms are—in other words, should it be a formal or casual presentation? You can then choose to follow those norms (and be seen as "fitting in") or choose to be different (and risk being seen as odd or rude . . . or creative and innovative). If it's a particularly creative field, you might want to go with the innovative approach. Follow these guidelines.

**Stick with your strengths.** This is not the time to try something new. Don't use a new technology. Don't arrange your notes a different way. Go with what you know works.

**Use your body to convey power.** Look your audience in the eyes. Gesture and speak slowly; walk around the entire space available.

**Keep it simple.** Create one compelling message. Unless required, try to keep visuals to a minimum.

**Know the goals of your speech.** Stay focused on your main points.

**Practice, practice, practice.** Enough said.

# mealtime interviews

**Don't be fooled into thinking the coast is clear**

Being taken to lunch by your future boss or colleagues, particularly when you are facing an entire day of interviews, may seem like common courtesy . . . and feel like a welcome relief to you. But don't kid yourself: The mealtime interview is a tried-and-true method of evaluation. Your dining partners are hoping to learn a lot about you.

■ How do you interact with strangers in a social setting?

■ Do you have good conversational and social skills? More than half of all business deals are finalized over meals, so these are critical skills to have.

■ Do you have good manners? Would you represent the company well during a meal with a client?

■ As you let your guard down, what is your true personality?

In the more friendly context of a meal, you may find that the conversation becomes more personal. You may be asked about your home life, hobbies, religion, politics, child care, or family history. But beware: These are illegal questions (see pages 58–59). Give only minimal information. Redirect the question back to whoever asks it. For example, if the interviewer asks about your babysitting arrangements, you might say, "I've never had child-care issues. What have you found works best?" Carefully choose your answer in light of how it affects your ability to do the job: Your dining partners will be listening carefully.

The good news is that being invited to lunch or dinner is a very positive sign. The bad news? You have to worry not only about what you say, but about the piece of lettuce that may be stuck between your teeth while you say it!

# Mealtime Manners

**Turn off cellular phones and pagers.**

**Open the door for your host.** Stand when being introduced to others.

**Follow your host's lead.** Sit down after she is seated. Make small talk until she is ready to order. If you are at a restaurant, wait for her to order first so that you can get an idea of how much and at what price range to order. If she gestures for you to go first, ask her, "What do you recommend?" Select something that isn't messy, unfamiliar, or difficult to tackle with a fork. If you are in a private company dining room, your choices are limited to just a few entrees (don't take more than your share, and be sure to thank the server).

**Don't start eating until your host does.**

**Don't gorge yourself,** but don't just pick at your food either: Not eating may signal that you can't handle social situations well.

**Eat with your mouth shut.** Still a cardinal rule.

**Avoid alcohol** even if your host has a drink.

**Don't make a big deal out of the bill.** Your host will probably take care of the bill, so don't keep insisting you'll pay for it.

**Use basic dining etiquette** regarding which fork you use and how you signal that you are finished eating. If you don't know the rules, learn them!

**If the food is not to your satisfaction**, eat what you can. It's not about the food, anyway.

**Don't smoke**, even if your host does.

Meals can also be highly informative. When you are dining with several people, colleagues may let their guard down, and you may:

**Hear valuable insider information** as the group starts talking shop. Listen for what they say about projects, competitors, other employees, organizational problems, and senior managers.

**Learn about their true personalities.** How they talk and what they talk about will give you a much clearer idea of whether you'd want to work with these people.

# long-distance interviews

## Traveling to be interviewed

During second-round interviews, you may have to travel to corporate headquarters to see the boss's boss, for example, or visit a regional office to meet the team you'll be supporting.

Some general guidelines when traveling:

**Check the travel schedule before you go.** Make sure the travel plans leave you plenty of room to arrive on time and are flexible enough to accommodate last-minute additions to the schedule or late-running interviews. If you think there might be a conflict, suggest some changes to the person making the travel arrangements.

**Pack for contingencies.** While it's great to pack light, you must be prepared for anything. Day trips may turn into overnights because the interview schedule gets extended or an interviewer isn't available until the next day. Different clothes may be required as new opportunities, such as a casual dinner out, come up. Calamities may happen: You spill coffee down your shirt or you get a run in your hose. Therefore, it's wise to pack an extra set of formal interview clothes and, if possible, a casual outfit.

Before you go, check all the details again. And don't forget to bring important materials, such as additional copies of your résumé, business cards, and your portfolio (see page 30).

# ASK THE EXPERTS

**I've just been asked to take a three-day trip to the company's West Coast office to interview with the director. Who is responsible for the travel expenses?**

Employers do not expect you to pay for out-of-town travel expenses such as airfare and hotels. If travel is fairly local (within an hour's drive), you'll probably be on your own for taxi, bus, or car expenses. But it's still smart to ask about this, particularly if you are facing multiple interviews and travel expenses start to add up.

Some expense guidelines when you are traveling out of town:

**Agree up front.** It is important to agree who will pay for what before you travel. What the company pays for can vary widely; for example, one organization may include a per diem allowance, while another won't. It also depends on how badly the company wants to recruit you, the candidate. The extent of the coverage gives you some insight into both the company and the strength of your candidacy.

**Clarify the process.** An organization will most likely want you to work through a travel agency it uses or an internal travel department. In either case, airline tickets, car service (with drivers to take you to and from the airport), and hotels may be arranged and paid for directly by the company. Usually you will put hotel fees on your credit card and be reimbursed later. Food is rarely covered.

**Save all your receipts.** They will be necessary for reimbursement and tax purposes. You cannot claim deductions for travel if you are interviewing for your first job or if you are switching careers. To find out more about what you can and cannot claim, head to **www.irs.gov**.

# videoconferencing

## Get ready to smile for the camera

Companies are increasingly turning to videoconferencing to screen candidates. This sophisticated technology allows companies to avoid travel costs by connecting you and the interviewer via a monitor, microphone, and video cable.

This is great if you wouldn't otherwise be able to meet a potential employer, but videoconferencing can be a little tricky. There's often a transmission delay and an echo that make conversation awkward. Speakers may overlap. You can't move around or you'll find yourself out of the camera's range. Don't panic. There are some tried-and-true ways to ace your video interview.

**Prepare ahead of time.** In addition to the general preparation you need to do for an interview, such as getting your success stories ready, you have to consider how the presence of a camera is going to affect things. Try to get the agenda ahead of time so that you can prepare your responses, and then get used to the process by practicing in front of a mirror or home videocamera.

**Keep it brief.** A videoconference interview is not as flexible as a face-to-face interview. Because of the time delay and the probable time limit on the interview, it won't have the easy give-and-take of a real dialogue. Keep your answers short, as you'll have no idea of your viewer's response—or whether he'll even be able to respond. If your viewer wants more information, he'll prompt you for it.

# Lights, Camera, Action!

If you've ever been on TV before, then you're a step ahead of others when it comes to videoconferencing. If this is your first time, don't let the presence of a camera make you nervous. Try to concentrate not on the fact that you're being filmed, but on the content of the interview itself. Here are some other ways to come across effectively on screen.

**Dress simply.** Solid primary colors work best. Don't wear blue or white: Both can disappear onscreen and leave you looking like a disembodied head. Avoid patterned clothing because it can "zigzag" on camera.

**Do not wear jewelry that glitters or makes noise.**

**If you normally wear eyeglasses, try to do the interview without them,** or wear contact lenses. The lenses in eyeglasses can reflect light and make it hard for an interviewer to see your eyes.

**Make sure your hair is pulled back** neatly off your face so that there are no shadows obscuring your eyes and facial expressions.

**Even if you don't normally wear makeup, do try and wear a bit** because a camera washes out facial features. Use face powder to reduce shininess; you don't want to look as if you're sweating from nervousness.

**Become familiar with the equipment.** Before you begin, test the microphone. Make sure the lights are as bright as possible so that the image will be clear. Ask to be shot from the waist up so that the viewer gets a good view of your face.

**Speak directly to the camera.** Avoid looking up, down, or to the side; it distracts the viewer.

**Remain still.** Sit with both feet on the floor and hands resting on a table so that you are well grounded. Try not to use too many hand gestures or fiddle nervously with your hair, a pen, etc.

**Speak slowly and clearly.** Wait until a question is asked completely before starting to answer because the time delay can throw things off.

# revisiting the hiring manager

**Your goal is to confirm that first positive impression of you**

As you move along the interview process, you'll probably find yourself facing the hiring manager or the person in charge of shepherding you through your second round of interviews. Use these encounters to further your case. This is a great time to ask for clarification about things you may have heard during your interviews with other people in the company. It's also a good time to further probe for the job's requirements and to state your qualifications and fit.

As you continue your visits, remain on your guard by being respectful, courteous, and aware of what you are revealing about yourself. At this point, the hiring manager may:

**Try to get your perspectives about the company.** As it becomes more likely that the company may hire you, the hiring manager may become concerned about whether you want to work there. He may ask your reactions to what you've seen so far or what you think about his team. These questions may arise from a sincere hope that you view the company favorably. They may also be a test of your candor and honesty.

**Revisit questions raised about your candidacy.** The hiring manager has most likely received assessments from everyone who has already interviewed you. If any red flags or doubts were raised, he will want to address them. Don't get defensive. Be thankful that he is giving you an opportunity to respond to his concerns. It is more damaging to your candidacy if he doesn't bring up concerns and instead just writes you off.

This is so important that instead of waiting for the hiring manager to bring up concerns, you can do it proactively by asking, "What did the interviewers think about my candidacy?" This gives him a chance to verbalize any concerns. He may also reveal key attributes that the company is looking for, and you can then expand on them. For example, if he says, "They said you are strong in analysis," tell him a success story that highlights that skill.

# ASK THE EXPERTS

## After meeting with a potential employer several times, I realize I really don't like the boss, but I still want the job. What should I do?

Never work for a jerk. No matter how attractive the job is, remember that you're going to be spending eight hours a day with this person. Those little irritating habits you notice now will balloon into things that drive you crazy later on. If it's a difference of morals or values, it's even more important to walk away from the job. Even if you delude yourself into thinking "I can handle him," your performance on the job will most likely suffer. That doesn't bode well for moving into a better position with a different boss. Besides, if the relationship falters, what kind of a recommendation will he give you?

It's very disappointing to have to say no to a fabulous job because of the boss. But lucky you! You figured that out before you accepted the job and started working for him. If you are still interested in the company, then you may want to return to HR or the original screeners and let them know you'd like to be considered for future openings. When the jerky boss gets fired, they may remember you and invite you back. The key is to not delude yourself: A jerk in the interview process is even more of a jerk on the job. Don't accept the job thinking you'll be able to cope with the situation or to change the boss.

## When do we discuss all the nitty-gritty stuff about a job?

Now is definitely the time. When you meet with the hiring manager again to review the interview process, you should ask questions that complete your picture of the job so you can make an informed decision. Questions to ask include:

■ What would you expect me to achieve in the first three months here?

■ When would my performance first be reviewed? How often thereafter?

■ What standards would my performance be measured against?

■ What kind of training and other resources are available to me?

# is it the right fit?

## Stop and picture yourself in this job

After going through what may feel like endless interviews, you may feel that, at last, a job offer is imminent. Now is the time to make sure all your questions have been asked. (See pages 62–63 for what to ask.) If those initial questions are answered to your satisfaction, then take some time to step back and ask yourself if you can really see yourself happy and thriving in this job.

**Skills.** If you clearly have the skills to do the job, will this job expand them? Will you be facing new challenges and responsibilities beyond your current experience? Will you have opportunities to learn about new skills, such as finance or marketing, in greater depth, adding to your expertise and further marketability? If not, will the company help you get outside training?

**Motivation.** What personal needs (the need for achievement, recognition, making a contribution, growth, etc.) would be met by the job? Would this job excite you over the long haul? How clear are the promotion opportunities and criteria for lateral transfers in this organization? How much does it matter to you?

**Fit.** Will your new boss and coworkers connect you to new opportunities and be pleasant to work with? Does your boss match your ideal in terms of communication and management style? If not, will you have opportunities to work with other senior staff?

**Reputation and values.** What is the reputation of the company in the marketplace? Will you be proud to say you work for this organization? Does the organization appear to demonstrate values that are consistent with yours? Are you comfortable with the company's culture? If it's a formal organization, for example, are you ready to wear a suit every day? If the company's culture is different from what you're used to, is there room for your own professional and personal style?

**Stability.** Will the company be around in five years? How vulnerable is the company to competitors edging it out of business? Will this job allow you to achieve the work/life balance that is important to you?

# ASK THE EXPERTS

**After I interviewed with everyone in the department, the hiring manager asked me about one particular coworker who I thought was a complainer. Should I tell her that?**

Definitely not! Chances are the hiring manager was the one who hired that complainer, so criticizing the colleague is criticizing the boss. There's a good chance the boss already knows the colleague is a poor performer—and that may be one of the reasons you are being hired. So stay positive and constructive anytime you are asked to give your opinion about one of the employees. At the very least, find one good characteristic to mention, then position yourself as filling in the gaps. For example, you could say, "I think George and I could work well together. He certainly knows a lot about our clients. I can add to that my teamwork skills and together we can tackle the challenges this department is facing."

**The negative things I've learned about the company make me question whether I'd want to work there. Should I voice my concerns?**

If you've done a good job analyzing the company and its people, you will inevitably identify some less-than-optimal aspects of working there. When the hiring manager asks what you think of the company, you may choose not to share negative impressions that are of minimal concern. But if your concerns are strong enough that you might reject a job offer, definitely tell the hiring manager. Avoid responding with a vague "It's too soon for me to tell." This usually tells him plenty: You avoid conflict, you're not candid, and you don't trust him. Instead, reveal your concerns in a noncritical way. Putting them in the form of a question positions you as a problem solver. For example, "A consistent message I'm getting that concerns me is that decisions are revisited and revised constantly. Can you tell me about that?"

# now what do I do?

## Answers to common questions

### I'm heading into a day of nonstop interviews. How do I survive?

A whole day of interviewing can be physically and mentally draining. To survive, not to mention enjoy, the process, you need to pace and fuel yourself. Here are some strategies.

**Make sure you eat.** Even if you're nervous, eat a good breakfast. Don't over-do it on the caffeine—chances are you'll be hyper enough from anxiety! If it's a full day, most employers will set up a lunchtime interview. But to make sure you can sustain your energy, stick a few granola bars in your briefcase.

**Take a break.** The savvy employer will schedule time in the day for you to be alone and gather your thoughts. If he hasn't, it's perfectly okay to ask for 15 minutes here and there as you need it.

**Take notes.** After two or three interviews, it can become very difficult to remember who said what. To keep all the conversations from blending togeth-er, either ask each interviewer for permission to take some notes during the conversation or jot down key points right after each interview. Noting what was said by you and the interviewer will also enable you to personalize thank-you notes later and pick up the conversation in follow-up interviews.

### I was just asked to come in and "work" for a day. Is this normal?

No, it's not. But it does happen more frequently in entry-level jobs, when you don't have the experience to show you have the skills. And it's common in some hands-on professions, such as teaching.

A working interview is a more thorough way of testing your probable per-formance once on the job. Some examples: Candidates for a teaching job spend a day in the classroom (earning a substitute teacher's wages); a paralegal is asked to proofread legal documents; a pastry chef creates desserts in the restaurant's kitchen; a journalist attends a town meeting and writes an article about it. In one instance, a senior-level HR candidate was asked to facilitate the senior management team in a four-hour strategic planning session. She was not paid for her time.

Another purpose is to see whether you fit in at the organization. You may be asked to work side by side with a potential coworker or to attend an account managers' meeting to brainstorm client issues.

The word "working" doesn't imply that you'll be paid for your time. Decide whether you think you should be compensated, then negotiate for what you believe the work is worth. If you feel the request is one that takes advantage of you, then try to negotiate a more reasonable demonstration of your skills.

## I've been called back for a second interview. When should I bring up the subject of benefits?

You should not bring up benefits until a job offer is made. If you are curious about a company's typical benefits package, you can try to do some research ahead of time; some companies post general information about employee benefits packages on their Web sites. Or, if you know someone who works for the company, you can try asking him or her.

# now where do I go?

**BOOKS**

**I Could Do Anything If I Only Knew What It Was**
by Barbara Sher

**Wishcraft: How to Get What You Really Want**
by Barbara Sher

**Do What You Are**
by Paul Tieger and Barbara Barron-Tieger

**Thought Leaders: Insights on the Future of Business**
by Joel Kurtzman

**The Brand You 50: Or: Fifty Ways to Transform Yourself from an Employee into a Brand that Shouts Distinction, Commitment, and Passion**
by Tom Peters

**Understanding Work Trends: We Are All Self-Employed**
by Cliff Hakim

**Chapter 8**

# evaluating and negotiating offers

# getting the offer

**Get ready to put negotiating skills into action**

Finally! You've been told over the phone or called in to get the great news: You got the job! Congratulations. But don't jump up, hug the hiring manager, and yell, "Yes!" Even if you are certain you want the job, take a few moments and realize that this job offer most likely comes with a lot of contingencies that you can negotiate, starting with your salary and including benefits, vacation days, overtime pay, etc. Remember that you're under no obligation to accept an offer as is, and that once you get the offer, it's perfectly okay to ask for time to think about it.

It's important to realize that at the beginning of the negotiation process you and the employer are somewhat at cross-purposes. The goal of an organization is often to bring employees in at the low end of a salary range, and then reward excellent performance by moving someone to the top of the range. Your goal, on the other hand, should be to come in at the middle or top of the range and, through outstanding performance, move into a new position and title with a higher salary range.

But even though you and the employer have different aims, it's really a win-win situation. And the fact that the company has said it wants you gives you the upper hand. Employers will rarely offer you everything they have to offer. This is why you need to be prepared to negotiate—and employers expect that you will. Failure to do so will have a short- and long-term impact on your finances, since raises are often percentage increases of a current salary. And it can affect how you're perceived in the organization, since how you conduct yourself as you negotiate and accept an offer often signals how you will manage relationships once inside the organization.

Your goal is to speak up for yourself without appearing greedy or unrealistic about your market value. With this in mind, take some time to fill in the offer evaluation worksheet at right to see how your needs and expectations might differ from your prospective employer's. This will help you kick off the negotiation process with a reasonable counteroffer.

# Offer Evaluation Worksheet

Use this worksheet to compare your goals with the employer's offer.

|  | MY GOAL | EMPLOYER'S OFFER |
|---|---|---|
| **Salary range** | | |
| ■ Aspire to | | |
| ■ Content with | | |
| ■ Live with | | |
| **Benefits** | | |
| ■ Health insurance | | |
| ■ Retirement plans | | |
| ■ Amount of annual vacation | | |
| ■ Other priorities for me | | |
| **Bonuses and other perks** (amounts and when) | | |
| ■ Signing bonus | | |
| ■ Year-end bonus | | |
| ■ Performance-based bonus | | |
| ■ Commission percentage | | |
| ■ Stock options | | |
| **Performance reviews** | | |
| ■ Date of first one | | |
| ■ Frequency after first one | | |

# salary concerns

**Examine salary surveys to get a sense of where you stand**

The first thing your future employer will put on the table is your salary. Is it what you thought it would be? Is it in keeping with your industry? Getting good information about salaries can be tough. To collect good information about your value in the marketplace, you may have to do some detective work.

Just how important is it to get this information ahead of time? It's important enough that you can actually lose a job offer if your salary request is considered outrageous. To take an example: A job seeker who moved to a rural area didn't adequately lower his salary expectations. When he asked for considerably more money than the original offer, the employer withdrew the offer because there was no way the company could even come close to this request. A more common occurrence is that people "leave money on the table," an expression that means the employer was willing to pay more but the employee didn't ask for it.

There are two ways to learn more about your value in the marketplace.

**Research salary surveys for your profession and geographic area.** There is a learning curve to using these databases, so figure out how to use them before you need the information. On page 165 you'll find some good Web sites for getting started.

**Talk to friends, colleagues, recruiters, and headhunters—** anybody who knows something about your industry—and ask about salary ranges for your type of work. Describe the job for which you are applying and ask, "What would you expect the salary range to be for such a position?" Then combine estimates, and check these against the salary surveys.

Observe one cardinal rule when talking with people about salaries: Never ask people what they make. Always ask about the salary range for a specific type of work. You can also try asking them if they know the salaries of coworkers who are doing the kind of job you're trying to land.

# **A** SK THE EXPERTS

## At what salary level do I have to be before I can start negotiating?

Research shows that positions paying less than $25,000 per year are usually assigned a specific hourly or yearly salary figure that is nonnegotiable. Why? Because there are many people who would be glad to fill these positions.

Mid-level positions that pay between $35,000 and $85,000 per year usually have a negotiating range. One recruiter at a large health-care organization reports a $2,000 range for mid-level positions, while an HR representative at an academic institution reports a $5,000 range for mid-level jobs. Positions paying more than $85,000 per year have the most flexibility for negotiation because these jobs often require specialized skills and years of experience, and fewer people are qualified for them.

## There's a space for my current salary on a job application form. I don't want to give that information. How should I handle this?

Know that an application with your signature on it is a legal document. Always be truthful on such forms. In fact, when prospective employers check references, they can ask about your salary. While you want to be honest, however, you don't want to undermine yourself. In your situation, you could leave the space blank.

Then, in the interview, you might say, "To get into this business, I came in with a salary below industry levels, and that was okay then. Now I have the skills and experience to expect compensation at market rates. From what I understand, that rate would be somewhere in the vicinity of . . ." (and give a wide range).

# analyzing benefits

**Good benefits can fill the gap when a salary offer is less than ideal**

Sometimes employers have little room to negotiate salaries. If that's what you're facing, then think about various benefits that might sweeten the pot for you and yet not cost the organization too much. Take some time and learn what types of benefits are available and whether you can put them on the table. Where do you find this information?

**Visit the Web site of your prospective employer.** Many organizations post a huge amount of information on their Web sites, and in the jobs section they may go into detail about standard benefits. Also, once you've received an offer, it's appropriate to ask for written materials that explain the organization's standard benefits package.

**Talk with colleagues at similar organizations to learn the industry standards**. For example, many large organizations pay for health insurance premiums or a substantial percentage thereof. But few startup companies provide such benefits. Getting inside information from others can help you be realistic about what to expect.

Once you have learned what the company has to offer, you can ask for additional benefits, such as telecommuting, especially if you think the benefits would help improve your work performance.

**RED FLAG**

Wait until an offer is on the table before talking about any benefits!

# Some Benefits to Think About Requesting

The following nonsalary benefits often show up on lists of requests made by employees. What would you add to this list? What four or five items are your top priorities?

support/resources for professional development

time off or funding for continuing education

equity in the company

stock options

earlier-than-normal first salary review

performance bonus

commission

signing bonus

overtime pay or days off in lieu of health insurance

financial planning assistance

home office equipment

home office expense reimbursement

paid membership(s) in professional group(s)

extra vacation time

flexible work hours

clothing allowance

company car

commuting allowance

travel insurance

401(k) plan

matching charitable donations

personal use of frequent flyer miles

flexibility to telecommute

optional leave of absence without pay

paternity, maternity, or family leave

working four 10-hour days rather than five 8-hour days

business-class travel on transcontinental trips

health club membership

relocation costs, including bridge mortgage for selling your current home and buying the next one

# negotiation in action

## Practical steps for negotiating effectively

So what does the negotiation process look like in action? Here's a typical scenario.

**Step one:** Either you or the employer puts a salary figure on the table. Who goes first? It depends. If you feel well prepared, then it's probably to your advantage to set the range first. If, however, you aren't sure how the position is valued in the marketplace, then it might be to your advantage for the employer to declare the salary range first.

**Step two:** Assume that the employer puts the salary figure on the table. What do you say? Nothing. Let silence follow. Then ask about the organization's standard benefits so that you will understand your total compensation package.

**Step three:** Address again the value that you'll bring to the organization and how much you'll be able to save the company. Then state a somewhat higher figure, along with any additional benefits you are requesting. Of course, be realistic and make sure your demands are well researched.

**Step four:** This is the employer's turn to make a counteroffer. You may be told that the company cannot go any higher on the salary but that it will support your wish to telecommute and, in fact, will set up a home office.

**Step five:** Pause again. This is a critical moment. You must decide how you will handle the salary issue apart from the rest of the package. If you do want the job regardless, you may ask when the organization conducts performance reviews. If the position allows you to set clear performance goals, then you might request a review in, say, three months rather than six. The implicit assumption is that you will receive a raise if you meet or exceed your performance goals.

**Step six:** The employer accepts your offer, or the process continues until you reach a verbal agreement. But before you give your final yes, ask for 48 hours to consider the offer. Then read the rest of this chapter for tips on making the most of an "offer in hand."

### Take Notes

Wherever you are in the negotiating process, remember to stay focused on your priorities; pause before you respond; listen carefully to the company's constraints; engage in give-and-take; and fight the urge to talk after you have given your requests. It's a good idea to bring a notebook and jot down the offers and counteroffers.

# Negotiation Lingo

**Opening position:** This is the first offer in a negotiation.

**Anchoring a negotiation:** The first figure put on the table generally sets the parameters for a negotiation. For example, if a prospective employer were to say that the salary range is between $58,000 and $60,000, then this most likely establishes your future salary. You may be able to bargain for a little over $60,000, but it's unlikely that you will shift the salary discussion to the $90,000 to $93,000 range.

**Best Alternative to a Negotiated Agreement (BATNA):** This is otherwise known as a "fallback position." In other words, if you cannot reach an agreement with the other side, what is your best alternative? For example, if you have pegged your value as between $75,000 and $85,000 and the prospective employer is offering $65,000, what do you say? If you have a better job offer, or BATNA, then you might decide to turn down the $65,000 job. Or, with a strong BATNA, you might negotiate more vigorously, since you have a fallback offer.

**Negotiating range:** This includes the low to high expectations in a negotiation. A range can encompass anywhere from a few thousand dollars for entry-level jobs to tens of thousands of dollars for executive-level ones.

**Deal breaker:** This is a point that one side will not concede or a requirement that is nonnegotiable.

**Counteroffer:** A change or concession from an original offer that is an attempt to reach a zone of agreement between the two parties.

**Concessions:** This is when one or both sides give up some of their demands to reach an agreement.

# negotiating tactics

## How to negotiate like a pro

If you've never negotiated for your salary, you're not alone. Negotiating is stressful, especially for first-timers. Take a deep breath and realize that once an offer has been made, you have nothing to lose by negotiating. All the employer can do is say no. Female candidates should pay special attention to negotiations since one of the main reasons women are paid less than men for similar work is that often women do not negotiate their salaries.

So, if you have never negotiated for your salary, it's time to take the following steps to put yourself on the road to higher pay and better benefits. Instead of saying "yes" or "thank you" when the offer comes, ask, "May I have time to think about that?" With that simple statement, you have signaled that you intend to bargain.

Once you have figured out what salary and range of benefits you would like, ask for a meeting. While you can negotiate over the phone, it's better to do the first round of negotiating in person.

**Don't be afraid to speak up.** Men often think of negotiating as a game. Women, on the other hand, often fear alienating others if they speak up. Know that you can advocate for yourself and still stay on good terms with the organization. In fact, negotiating well often strengthens relationships.

**Be prepared to wait for a response to your request.** Most likely the other side will need to check with several people within the organization to see how to respond to your request. And you should also know that taking time to respond is a standard negotiating tactic. When facing silence, you might be tempted to reduce your demands. Don't.

**Once the negotiation process is over, assess how well you did.** Did you get movement on one or two of your critical issues? Did the other side make statements such as "That's the top of our salary range"? If so, then it sounds as if you were successful. Congratulate yourself for beginning to develop one of life's critical skills.

## ASK THE EXPERTS

### I'm nervous about the idea of negotiating my salary. What can I do?

Take a course in negotiating. Many professional associations and universities offer everything from one-day programs to semester-long courses where you are taught negotiating principles and you role-play tough situations. A major advantage of these courses is that you receive feedback on your strengths and weaknesses as a negotiator, and this in turn can help you improve your skills.

## FIRST PERSON SUCCESS STORY

### Bargaining Power

The last time I was offered a job in my industry, I accepted the first offer that they put on the table. Later, I found out that all of my coworkers had started out with salaries at least $5,000 higher than mine. So I told myself that the next time around I would be much more aggressive. When I got my next job offer, I was tempted to accept it right away. It took a lot of courage for me to say I needed to think about the offer. I was afraid they'd change their minds! Then I did some quick research and found out that while this company paid some of the higher salaries in the business, they tended to skimp on benefits. And the more I read the fine print of their offer, the more I realized this was true. So I came back with a counteroffer that was $10,000 higher in salary and included every one of the benefits I was hoping to get. I figured I had nothing to lose. Though I didn't get the extra $10,000, they did give me most of the benefits I asked for and told me later they were impressed that I'd negotiated so well.

—Shannyn P., Yuma, Arizona

# bargaining bumps

## How to handle the turbulence

**D**on't be surprised if you encounter some bumps along the way. Some of these bumps may be major, such as being offered a much lower salary than you expected and being told "That's our final offer." Or they could be minor, such as being unable to agree on whether severance pay in the event of job termination should cover 6 or 12 months. What's a candidate to do?

Your first tactic is to pause and say, "Let me get back to you about that." If you have friends who are recruiters, headhunters, career counselors, or coaches, ask them for advice. They may have in-depth knowledge about pay scales, standard benefits, and hiring

procedures that will allow you to understand how the other side is thinking.

If you are asked to sign any documents, it's a good idea to run them by an employment lawyer. Employment lawyers can walk you through anything you don't fully understand. They can also advise you if you are asked to sign documents that make you uncomfortable, such as noncompete agreements, and can act on your behalf to get more information about these documents before you do sign.

People who are seeking executive-level or consulting positions may be asked to sign one or more of the following documents.

**An employment contract** usually runs 10 to 20 pages and outlines benefits, such as employee stock options and grounds for termination, in extensive detail.

**A noncompete agreement** stipulates that you will not work for competitors for a specific period of time after leaving a company.

**A confidentiality agreement** requires that you neither talk nor write about the work you are doing for a corporation, nor reveal the company's business strategy or any of its product information.

# ASK THE EXPERTS

## I just got two job offers at the same time. I'm interested in both jobs. What should I do?

This is a good thing, though some candidates find this happy situation very stressful because they now have to negotiate with two parties instead of one. Your first action should be to inform the first company of the other company's offer and ask them if they want to make you a better offer. If they do, you can then go to the other firm with it and see if they can improve their offer. If they really want to hire you, they will probably increase it. The important point here is that you have to know when to stop the bidding war—you don't want to play two companies off each other to the point that you lose both offers!

## How do I find a good employment lawyer?

The best way to find a good attorney is to ask for recommendations from people whose opinions you respect. Then call the attorneys and explain the kind of advice you are seeking. If they have experience in your field or industry, then ask about practical issues such as their fees and availability.

## How do I tell the employer I don't want the job after all?

If you have decided you don't want the job, then say so clearly, concisely, and as early on in the process as possible. Give an explanation—you have another offer, you don't want to move, or the pay is not high enough—but be brief and clear. Hold on to the relationships. There is a greater than 50 percent chance that you got into the interview and organization through a network of friends and colleagues. For the long-term health of your career, you want to maintain the goodwill and support of that network. Consequently, take your exit with grace.

# closing the deal

## Thank those who helped

You survived the negotiations and got offered nearly everything you wanted. Now what? You say yes. But before you broadcast this wonderful news, be sure you've been told when you are starting. If you need to take any tests for the job, make sure you pass them before you approach your current boss with your resignation. And if your new job requires any paperwork, such as a written agreement or an employment contract, wait until it has been approved.

Once everything is in order, contact your boss and tell her the news. Write it out in a letter of resignation or make an appointment and tell her in person. Either way be sure to thank her for employing you. Be cordial as you work out the details of your last days there. You are likely to continue to see this former boss at business and professional events, so try to remain on good terms. She may also still need to serve as a reference at some point in the future.

The other thing you need to do is make it a point to thank people who helped you land the new job.

**Human resources recruiter:** If a recruiter played a critical role in bringing you into an organization, then thank the recruiter in person or in a note.

**Your new boss:** Explicitly thank your new boss for hiring you and emphasize how much you look forward to working together.

**Your new boss's boss:** Often a short note will set the right tone.

**The network of friends and colleagues that helped you find your position:** Let the people who helped you during your job-hunting process know about your success. A succinct e-mail message keeps others informed and lets them celebrate with you. This also updates them with your new contact information and keeps you in their network.

# ASK THE EXPERTS

**My new boss wants me to start working immediately so I can pitch in on an important project. But I still need to give notice at my old job. What should I do?**

You want to start off on a good foot with your new employer, but asking you to start working before you've resigned from your current job is unreasonable. It may, in fact, be a test. If you dump your old job to start working for your new boss right away, he may worry that you'll do the same thing to him down the line.

What you can do, however, is volunteer to be "on call" for the new project—in other words, provide input by phone or e-mail until you're able to start full-time. Though you probably won't be paid for your time, your new boss will appreciate your commitment and support. If more substantial input is needed, you might try to schedule a meeting for a weekend to show that you are willing to jump in. Be sure to agree on compensation for this.

**When I received the written job offer, some things were different than what we agreed on verbally, such as the total number of vacation days (14 instead of 15). When I brought this up, the hiring manager said I had heard wrong. What do I do?**

Your new boss probably isn't trying to pull the wool over your eyes, although it's not unheard-of. The two of you simply have different recall of the conversation. Although you might worry that you'll be seen as argumentative if you bring up these discrepancies, you'll probably feel resentful if you don't, and this can affect your work. If you bring it up, your new boss may even think highly of you for being attuned to details.

In the best scenario, the hiring manager will realize that he made a mistake and correct it. In the worst scenario, you just won't get the extra day—he's not going to take the job offer away. This is why taking notes during the negotiation process is so valuable: If discrepancies arise, you can confirm what was agreed upon.

# now what do I do?

## Answers to common questions

### Once I have an offer, should I go back to my current employer and see whether the company wants to make a counteroffer?

There are plenty of reasons not to do that. First of all, most people don't leave their jobs because of money. It's usually dissatisfaction with the boss, the work, or the organization. Those things won't change with more money. It will also be tough to return to your current job after getting excited about a new one. Plus, you may not be trusted anymore: Once word is out that you're looking externally, you will lose your place in the inner circle.

### Can I negotiate for more vacation time?

Vacation time is often determined by organizational factors. Many organizations, for example, give new employees two weeks of vacation while people with seniority receive four weeks. Other organizations determine vacation by position in the hierarchy, with lower-level employees receiving less. If more vacation time is your top priority, then put the issue on the table. If both you and your prospective employer have a win-win attitude, then you may arrive at a creative solution for more time, even though that goes against the organizational norm. Don't be surprised, however, if the organization shows little flexibility with this issue.

### I've been offered a job that is more a lateral move than a vertical one. Should I take it?

The decision depends on many factors. If you'll develop new skills or a new area of expertise, then you might take the new position. If the move is into an organization that appeals to you more than your present one, take the new job. In a world of less hierarchical organizations, there is a need for people with cross-functional knowledge, so taking lateral moves is often smart.

### The title I have been offered is not what we discussed and I don't think it reflects the level of responsibility for the job. What now?

Talk to the hiring person about your impression that the title does not match the level of responsibility. Since job titles are not consistent across organizations, it's possible your impression is incorrect, especially if the compensation is close to what you want. If your impression is correct, the next step is to try to negotiate a better title. If there is a win-win attitude, then you should be able to fix this problem. If you cannot reach an agreement, however, ask yourself whether you will be frustrated and resentful in the new position. If the answer to that question is yes, then turn down the job.

## I have two offers: one for a lot of money at a small startup and one for less money at a more established company. Which is the better offer?

First, gather information about the two companies. What is the financial condition of the small company? What's the chance that it will be sold soon? You need to do your due diligence on the company and see what its future holds in the coming three to five years.

Gather information on the more established company. What is its financial condition? Who are its competitors? What new products or services does it have in the marketplace? Might this company be bought or sold soon? Do your due diligence on this company, too. The next step is to go over your list of priorities (see page 151). What are the four or five factors that are most important to you? While you mention only two considerations, the two organizations are likely to differ in a number of different ways. Make a list of pluses and minuses for each company on as many different dimensions as you can imagine, and then make your decision.

# now where do I go?

**In-depth company profiles:**

www.hoovers.com

**Web sites with salary information:**

www.rileyguide.com
This is the mother lode of Web sites dealing with employment and job search issues.

www.salary.com
Personal salary reports can be purchased.

www.careerjournal.com
This *Wall Street Journal* career site has good salary guides and articles on negotiation and severance packages.

www.jobstar.org
Largest collection of salary surveys online.

www.bls.gov
Government site that provides useful, but sometimes outdated, information.

**Finding professional associations:**

The American Society of Associations
www.info.asaenet.org/gateway

**Negotiating courses:**

Harvard University Law School
Semester-long courses, Program on Negotiation (PON):
www.law.harvard.edu/programs

Short programs:
www.pon.execseminars.com

Simmons College School of Management (SOM)—negotiating programs for women:
www.simmons.edu/som/executive

American Management Association—offers a short course on developing negotiating skills:
www.amanet.org/seminars

Chapter 9

# reviving a stalled job search

# overcoming rejection

## Mourn the loss and move on—quickly

You got through the telephone interview but didn't make the next cut. Or you made it all the way to the final round and didn't get the job. Both situations are painful. You know that you need to reenergize your interview process, but it can be hard to do after a setback. You may never know exactly why you didn't get the job. But you can reflect on the interview process and try to figure out what might have tripped you up.

**Organizational issues:** Sometimes organizations go on "fishing expeditions," in which they interview people to see who is on the market. The organization is in a position to hire if it finds the perfect candidate, but if it doesn't, it'll stop the search. Or an organization's business takes a downturn and it decides not to hire. Or the strategic direction of an organization shifts, and the posted position no longer matches the critical needs of the organization. For a variety of internal reasons, organizations sometimes decide not to hire, and it has little or nothing to do with how you performed on the interview process.

**Interview issues:** You need to be honest with yourself about whether something you did or said may have tipped the interviewer against you. There are three main reasons for not making the cut:

**1.** You were either over- or underqualified for the job.

**2.** You were ambivalent about wanting the job and/or doubted your abilities to perform it.

**3.** The chemistry was not right between you and one of the interviewers. Often, more than one of these issues is at play when you do not make the next cut.

How do you figure out where the problem lies? Ask for feedback. If you don't make the cut after a phone interview, call the interviewer back and ask why. Same goes for in-person interviewers. While some may find this conversation uncomfortable, you can ease their concerns by asking the right questions. You might first wish them sincere good luck with the person they hired, express a continued interest in the organization, and then say, "It would be helpful if you could let me know what about my performance or background might not have been the right fit."

# How to Get Feedback

Before you refocus yourself and your job hunt, go back to those who rejected you and ask for feedback. Here are some sample questions you can ask.

### Do you think I was underqualified for the job?

If you hear from more than one potential employer that you are underqualified, listen up. Then either make a better pitch for your application or apply for jobs that are more in line with your qualifications.

### Do you think I was overqualified for the job?

If a potential employer replies that yes, you seem overqualified, then you should do two things. First, ask him to keep you in mind for future positions that are more suitable to your background, then regularly check for openings with the company if it's one you really want to work for. Second, if you really do want to take a job at this level (for example, if you are switching industries and feel that you need to start out lower on the ladder), then next time you apply for a similar position, try to shape your résumé and cover letter to emphasize why a company would benefit from hiring such a qualified person for this position.

### I'm just curious, but I was wondering if my enthusiasm for the job came across in the interview?

If an employer replies that you did not seem particularly interested in the job, you should reflect on what you really want in a job and in that particular organization. It's possible that upon reflection you'll find you really didn't want the job in the first place.

Now that you've heard the reasons for not making the grade, give yourself some time to recover. We've all heard the saying "Get right back on the horse!" This is admirable to do, but don't feel that you need to do it immediately. Acknowledge that you are disappointed, are tired, were treated unfairly, or whatever the case may be. Then brush yourself off and try again.

# mirror, mirror on the wall

**Learning to see yourself as others see you**

Okay, so you realize there was a problem with your interview. Now you need to consider your behavior during the interview. Did you do anything to turn off a prospective employer? Did you sound less interested in the job than you really were? Developing self-awareness of how your behavior is seen by others is critical if you want to improve your interviewing skills.

Here are a few methods for developing self-awareness.

**The mirror.** Sit down in front of a mirror with your prepared answers to commonly asked interview questions. Then, give your answers just as if you were in an interview. How do you look when you answer these questions? Do you do anything odd or annoying, or do you look self-confident and eager to get to work? Would you want to hire the person whom you're facing?

**The audiotape.** Turn the tape recorder on and respond to common interview questions, then listen to yourself. Do you hesitate before you answer questions? Do you use a lot of *hmms*, *ahhhs*, or other sound-fillers? Or is your tone self-confident and strong?

**The videotape.** Turn on your videocamera and record yourself as you conduct your mock interview. How do you look? How do you sound? What can you do to improve?

**Practice in front of friends or relatives.** You can count on family and friends to be critical and tell you what you're doing wrong. Another good reason to practice with friends and family is that they want you to land that job as much as you do, so they'll do their best to provide helpful feedback.

Perhaps you might even switch roles with a friend who knows you so well that she is able to take your role while you become the interviewer. It's amazing how much you might learn by listening to what you "could" sound like.

# Hiring a Career Counselor

Another way to evaluate your interviewing skills is to hire a professional career counselor. Hearing yourself explain your accomplishments and respond to questions can be valuable, as can the feedback of a trained professional. Think of your career counselor as part expert, part coach. While there are a number of people out there claiming to be job counselors, you want to hire someone who has been certified by your state to be a career counselor.

Fees for career counseling usually range from $50 to $100 an hour, much like the fees for personal counseling. (There should be no up-front payments or contracts requiring you to commit to a course of payments.) If money is an issue, a less expensive option is the group sessions offered by some counselors. These groups meet regularly to work on interviewing skills. Note: If you have been laid off from a company, your outplacement benefits may include professional career counseling.

The best place to find a qualified career counselor is with the organization that certifies career counselors: the National Board for Certified Counselors. Call 336-547-0607 or contact the organization through its Web site, **www.nbcc.org**. Representatives can help you find a certified counselor in your area.

# joining a job seekers group

## Work with a group of fellow job hunters

One of the best methods for improving your interviewing skills is to work with a group of fellow job seekers. This can help you in several important ways.

First is in the area of feedback. With a group of people who are facing the same issues day in and day out, you will be able to explain what happened and get suggestions from the group about how they might have handled the situation differently.

A second important function of a job seekers group is to help you hold yourself accountable for the progress that you're making in the interview process. Well-run groups meet on a regular basis, usually once a week. During the meeting you announce your goals, and the following week you report on whether or not you met them. If you did, then you might set more aggressive goals for the following week. If you didn't meet your goals, then the group will challenge you to examine your behavior. What did you do to undermine your effectiveness? How can you do better next week?

The third important function of a group is to provide support. As you probably know by now, job hunting can be an isolating experience. A job seekers group can provide needed support and social interaction during the interview process.

The fourth function is to generate ideas. Interacting with a group of 6 to 10 people who are engaged in the same activity as you are will expand your knowledge of the job search process. One person might learn about a useful Web site, while another person might hear that a major corporation is once again hiring and pass that information along to the group. You get the idea: Sharing and exchanging ideas will increase your sophistication about how to interview effectively.

# ASK THE EXPERTS

### How do I find a job seekers group?

Search out job seekers groups run by nonprofit organizations such as colleges and churches. For example, a college might invite alumni to a weekly job seekers meeting, or a church may have established a group for members of the community when there was a serious down-turn in the economy. Check your local newspaper and talk with other job hunters to see what is available in your community.

Try a for-profit job search group. One of the oldest for-profit job support groups is the Five O'Clock Club. Founded by Kate Wendleton, author of several books on career management, this club is virtual and links members via telephone and e-mail. In some of the larger cities, such as New York and Chicago, there are face-to-face meetings for job searchers. The fee for career coaching is based on a sliding scale. Visit **www.5occ.com**.

Some state unemployment insurance offices arrange groups for job hunters. Go to your local unemployment insurance office and ask if this service is provided. Or visit **www.rileyguide.com** and search by your state and locality. Ask government personnel to recommend a job support group if the unemployment insurance office doesn't run one.

### I haven't been able to find a group that deals with the problems of being laid off, so I'd like to start one. How do I go about it?

If you are going to create your own job seekers group, there are four operating principles you should abide by. First, establish a consistent time, place, and duration for the meeting. Second, be clear about the structure and purpose of the meeting. For instance, you will discuss ways to get a job for an hour, then socialize for half an hour. Third, decide how you will handle membership. Is this a drop-in group for all who are job hunting, or is it a closed-membership group? If it's the lat-ter, then you should have approximately 7 to 10 people as members. Fourth, stay focused on the business at hand. If people do not learn tac-tics to help them in their job search, they will stop coming to the group.

# making things happen

**When it's time to take things up a notch**

You've answered countless ads by companies offering jobs and you've sent out countless résumés. For whatever reason, neither HR managers nor HR recruiters are begging to interview you. If this is what you're facing, don't lose heart; get creative and proactive. There are several ways to put yourself on an employer's radar and gain valuable interview and job experience while you're at it.

**Employment agencies:** These are independent firms, often specializing in particular careers or industries, that maintain databases of qualified job seekers. Companies often contract with employment agencies to locate the right person to fill a job opening. If you want to get your foot in the door of a large company, consider going through an employment agency.

**Temporary placement firms:** If you're looking to switch careers or build experience, a temporary placement can be a great way to enhance your résumé. And it's not uncommon for a temporary placement to lead to a permanent one.

**Job fairs:** At these large, day-long events, organizations may conduct brief first-round interviews for current openings. Attending job fairs is also a good way to learn about an industry.

**Informational interviews:** These are brief introductory meetings that you schedule with key staff at organizations that interest you. Even if there are no job openings, this is an excellent strategy for making employers aware of you.

No matter which option you pursue, interviewing with employment agencies or temporary placement firms can be just as important as interviewing with a future boss. Ready to get moving? Pick up the phone and set up an interview, or start searching the newspaper for an upcoming job fair in your area.

# Tips for Interviewing with Screeners

Interviews at job fairs and interviews with executive recruiters or temporary agencies are ways of "screening" potential employees. (See page 15.) Though the people who interview you, known as screeners, may not be able to land you the job, they can serve as an important link to the employer, so treat their interviews seriously. If you do get the green light to interview with a screener:

**1.** Make sure you're prepared. If it's an informational interview or job fair, study up on the organization(s) before you go in.

**2.** Practice articulating your position statement and success stories until they are second nature and can be shaped to fit several questions.

**3.** Figure out how you can help screeners help you. Make sure they have all the information they need to present you as a strong candidate to the decision makers.

**4.** Regardless of whether you find them helpful or not, respect all the screeners you encounter. Being arrogant or condescending may get you zapped further down the hiring road.

**5.** Ask for feedback. While there are legal limits to the amount of information screeners can provide, what they can give you could help you figure out how to be a stronger candidate.

**6.** Stay in the present. Focus on this one interview, this one question. Don't think too far ahead by asking yourself, for example, whether you'll really like this job.

**7.** Lighten up. Have fun talking with screeners and the variety of people you meet during the interviewing process. If you engage screeners from the beginning, they might be more willing to help you further down the line.

# employment agencies

**It's fairly easy to get a first-round interview with them**

Employment agencies generally fill entry- and mid-level jobs. No doubt you've seen their ads in the newspapers. Those ads are usually very open-ended, for example, "Wanted: Office assistant to help in busy publishing office. Must be organized, have computer skills, and be able to file." The employer is never specified; rather there is a contact name of a person at an employment agency.

Some agencies work on commission; others are on a retainer. Their goal is to build a database of job seekers so as to readily fill positions when a job request comes in. Scan through the newspaper and pick only those agencies that match your career interests and experience, then call them and introduce yourself. If you fit what they're looking for, you will most likely be able to arrange an interview. Prepare for an employment agency interview just as intensely as you would for a hiring organization interview (see Chapter 2). Remember, the agency screener has the names and telephone numbers of hiring managers, and it's her job to pass along the credentials of qualified job seekers like you.

Also keep in mind that there will be some kind of side communications going on between the agency and the company about you. While there is no way to know what is being said, you can try and hypothesize about how you might stack up against some of the other candidates whom the agency is recommending for the same position. Though you will not have specifics, just try to be savvy. If you are called back for a follow-up interview with the company, make sure to keep the agency in the communication loop about this development.

Why do companies use employment agencies? There are a number of good reasons. One is that the hiring organization does not want to increase its own human resources staff, since its hiring needs constantly change. Another reason is that the hiring organization does not want its present employees to know that it's seeking outside employees. Another possibility is that the employment agency has access to people with specialized skills and the hiring organization needs such people immediately.

# Five Questions to Ask Employment Agencies Before You Interview with Them

**1.** Before you walk into an employment agency's office, call and ask who pays the fees for its services. About 80 percent of the time the hiring organization pays the fees. Do not deal with an agency that requires you to pay for its services. Period. There are too many options available to you for free.

**2.** Ask the agency whether it specializes in an industry and/or function. For example, some agencies focus on the financial services industry, others handle hiring only for health care organizations, and still others work with a wide range of industries. In contrast, some agencies specialize in a function, such as technology, across all industries. Work only with an agency whose specialty matches your career interests.

**3.** Ask what type of placement the agency conducts for various organizations, and know what you are seeking. The possibilities include permanent jobs, temporary to permanent placement, and temporary jobs only.

**4.** Ask the agency whether it specializes in entry- or mid-level jobs or a certain salary level. This way, you won't waste your time working with an agency that cannot meet your requirements. For example, if you are just starting out in your field, an employment agency that places only managers or employees commanding more than $50,000 per year will not want to work with you.

**5.** If there is time and the person you are speaking to seems happy to continue the discussion, ask whom the agency's clients are and how long the agency has worked with them. Employment agencies can be useful to you when they have strong working relationships with hiring managers within organizations. Agencies that have worked with an organization for two or more years have a strong partnership.

# temporary placement firms

## How to get a head start in your field

**W**hile you're waiting for the phone to ring, why not work? How? Enter the world of temporary employment. It's a great way to make money, gain valuable experience, get your foot in the door, and expand your job contact network. There are a number of temporary employment agencies (also known as temp agencies) that hire people to work for anywhere from 1 to 10 weeks at the offices of their corporate clients. These jobs can be anything from office assistant to tax accountant.

Here's how it works: Say you are a terrific office assistant who has worked in retail for five years. You've just been laid off. If you sign up with a temp agency, you may be assigned to work as an assistant at a bank for two weeks, followed by another assignment as an office aid at a busy legal firm. It all depends on what's available

and what you're interested in taking. The bank would then pay the temp agency, which in turn pays you.

Here is another good reason to consider temping. Employers get to see your fine skills in action. If they like what they see, they might hire you for a permanent position. It used to be that these firms worked only with people who held low-level jobs in corporations. Not anymore. Since the early 1990s the use of temporary employees has been a significant, and ever growing, part of the American employment market. Surprisingly, the fastest-growing segment of all temporary employment is **white-collar staff,** people who hold executive, managerial, and professional positions.

# How to Get onto the Rosters of Temporary Placement Firms

**1.** Call and introduce yourself, then send in a résumé. Ask the agency representative whether she prefers a hard-copy resume, an e-résumé, or both.

**2.** Expect a call from the firm. If you do not hear from the agency within two weeks, call and request an interview.

The level of economic activity often drives whether or not you'll go in for an interview. If the economy is hot and unemployment is low, then the firm will most likely invite you in for an interview. If economic activity is slow and unemployment is rising, the staff will invite you only when the need for your skills arises.

**3.** If invited, go in for an interview. Expect to fill out application forms before the interview. Since résumés are not legal documents, some firms view their applications as legal documents and require you to sign and date your papers before you talk with anyone. Be prepared to deal with the issues of salary and references on application forms. Fill out all parts of the application honestly. Since a firm's relationship with its clients depends on your ability to perform as stated, it usually checks every aspect of your application.

**4.** During the interview, explain clearly your specific set of skills and what kinds of tasks you can complete masterfully.

**5.** Prepare to take tests that measure your skills. For example, if you are interviewing to fill temporary editing positions, expect to take tests to measure your editing skills. If you work in administrative or secretarial positions, be prepared to take tests on specific office skills such as spreadsheets or word processing.

## RED FLAG

There should be no charge for any tests or job placements. If a temp agency says there are fees you need to pay to get on its list, leave.

# job fairs

## First-round interviews on the spot

**J**ob fairs are often sponsored by major city newspapers. The newspaper invites all the organizations that pay to run want ads in its employment section. In metropolitan areas, these fairs tend to be large, with 200 organizations attending. The participating companies bring information about themselves and make screeners available. They may be interviewing for specific jobs or they may just be looking to build a database of candidates.

**Specialized job fairs** cater to specific areas of the employment market. For example, there are job fairs for hospital workers and for teachers. Specialized job fairs tend to reflect the labor markets for which an area is known. Silicon Valley in California, for instance, has high-tech job fairs, as does Boston.

**Career fairs** at colleges and universities are another type of job fair. Here college students and alumni can find out about various corporations that are keen on recruiting new college grads.

What types of job fairs occur in your area? Check out the want-ads section of your major newspaper or its Web site for a listing. If the fairs do not match your industry or functional interest, then consider attending fairs in other cities.

Different job fairs tend to screen for different job levels. Often the large, general job fairs attract recruiters with entry-level positions. The specialized job fairs tend to bring in recruiters seeking functional specialists and candidates for upper-level positions.

Once you get to the fair and are standing in front of the screener, what next? You have 30 seconds to deliver your statement of what you are looking for to a recruiter who has already met 200 other people that day. The good news is that you are having a one-on-one conversation with a screener from a company that interests you. The bad news is that this recruiter needs to remember you tomorrow morning when he turns in the hundreds of résumés he will collect at this fair.

# Prepare a 30-Second Pitch

At a good job fair, there will be a lot of activity. You need to be able to capture the attention of a screener fairly quickly. One way to do that is to prepare a 30-second job pitch. This pitch should be short but compelling. Some call this an **elevator speech,** i.e., what you might say to a human resources manager if you were riding the elevator together.

It's composed of three key items.

**1.** A statement about a future goal or skill you have

**2.** A mini-illustration of how you have achieved that goal or skill in the past

**3.** A request for information about jobs that would use those skills

Here is an example of a short job pitch: "My goal is to design Web sites for an educational institution. I have a knack for instructional technology. The project that I'm most proud of included a team of middle school and high school science teachers. We developed a Web site that gave students a better understanding of the life cycle of frogs. Are there people in your institution that might need the passion and skills of a dedicated instructional technology person such as myself?"

Here's another example: "I used to work for ____ Corporation. I was part of the team that developed a platform for a macromedia product. But what I'm really interested in is instructional technology. I tried to move over to the eLearning team when our project ended, but they weren't hiring. What's going on at your company? Is it interested in upgrading the tech skills of its employees? If so, then I could be of help."

# informational interviews

**Okay, they're not with "official" screeners, but they can help**

The informational interview is often overlooked by job seekers, but this kind of interview can be invaluable. In an informational interview, you contact people at organizations that interest you, and ask to meet with them briefly to learn more about their work. This has the twofold effect of introducing you to potential employers and helping you gain knowledge about a particular industry. While this won't always lead to a job right away, it's a good way of making your presence known so that if your dream job does open up at an organization, you just may get the call.

To get started, ask friends or colleagues for names of people to call at organizations where you would like to work. Make sure you do considerable research on these organizations and prepare questions ahead of time. Limit your informational interviews to only a few firms, the ones you are most interested in and knowledgeable about.

Call or e-mail the designated person and request a reasonable amount of time for an informational interview. The less well connected you are to the person, the less time you should request. This type of interview usually lasts 15 to 30 minutes. Although it's only a brief interview, treat it as you would any other, and be as professional and courteous as possible.

When you meet the informational interviewee, make sure to stick to the allotted time. Ask your most important questions first, since your time could run out. And do your best to convey your talents and experience in a concise, articulate way.

At the end, ask, "Who else would you suggest I speak with?" If the interviewee doesn't want to give you any names, thank him and leave. If the people you interview are constantly forwarding your résumé and giving you further contacts, then you're doing fine. If, on the other hand, few people are willing to give you names, then you need to assess what you're doing wrong (see pages 170–171).

# ASK THE EXPERTS

### What questions should I ask at an informational interview?

You want to ask questions about the person giving you the interview to learn more about the industry. To that end, you can ask:

How did you become interested in this industry?

What training did you find helpful?

What do you do now?

What do you like about it?

How would you suggest someone go about trying to get a job in this field?

### I've tried setting up an appointment to meet with this one person for an informational interview, but she keeps canceling. What should I do?

Chances are your person is very busy, and your request is being granted only out of the goodness of her heart or as a favor to someone who knows you. When dealing with a busy person, be patient. If all else fails, ask if it would be okay to e-mail your questions to her. Perhaps you can suggest a more neutral place to meet outside the office that might be convenient for a busy person.

## FIRST PERSON SUCCESS STORY

### Financial Fit

After earning a degree in accounting, I thought for sure I wanted to work for one of the big financial firms. After sitting through several informational interviews, however, I realized that the hard-core corporate environment was really not my style. In the end, I took a position as the financial manager for a modern dance troupe, which was much more my speed. (And it's a great way to get free tickets to cultural events!) In retrospect, the informational interviews were really valuable in helping me figure out what I didn't want to do.

—Aaron J., Los Angeles, California

# now what do I do?

## Answers to common questions

### I'm not really interested in the jobs I'm qualified for. What should I do?

Get an objective evaluation of yourself and your talents by taking some standardized personality tests. These allow you to compare yourself to others and gain self-knowledge through your answers. One of the most popular of these is the Myers-Briggs Type Indicator, which reveals your true working personality. You can access the test and explanations of your score at **www.mbti.com**. Once you have your score and have analyzed it, you might find that your talents lie in another field or area than the ones you've been working in. You might want to consider a career change and go back to school for training, or you might want to consider a skill change, such as going from customer relations to working as a corporate in-house troubleshooter.

### I wasn't allowed to interview for a position because the screener said a writing sample that I submitted didn't look professional. Can she do that?

By law employers must link their interviewing and selection process directly to the requirements of the job. Employers must also ask for the same materials from all applicants. If the writing sample was directly connected to the job that you would have performed, and if this screener asked everyone for a writing sample, then she was within the scope of her job to reject your application based on your writing sample. Ask someone who is knowledgeable in your field to check over the document you intend to submit and to give you feedback.

### I've read that there is a growing need for interim corporate managers. Would this be a good way to get a permanent job?

Doing temporary work in an organization is an excellent way to find out whether there is a good match between your values and those of the organization. This also gives a company the opportunity to closely assess you and your skills. When there is a downturn in the economy, the trend toward outsourcing and using temporary managerial workers increases. For example, performers with skill sets such as accounting and finance are in growing demand, with many companies coming under the scrutiny of regulators and therefore needing extra assistance. With the right set of skills, you could transition yourself into a new permanent job.

## I've spent the past 20 years raising three kids. How can I get back into the corporate working world?

Volunteer for a reputable nonprofit organization whose mission matches your values and whose work is related to your field of interest. Figure out what kind of work you want to do and contact several organizations to see how you might help them. Most likely, you'll be able to find a position that requires only a few hours each week but that puts you in contact with people who can help you when you want to get a job.

Join professional associations and become an active member. Most professional organizations have a large number of members who pay their dues and do little else. You, on the other hand, can become an active member by going to meetings, volunteering to lead special projects, and connecting with people who work in organizations that interest you. As you show your commitment to the association and this industry, people will notice you. If you are open to doing project work, make sure you let people know. The more people who know and respect your work, the more likely you'll get a job.

# now where do I go?

## WEB SITES

### www.kennedyinfo.com
Kennedy Information publishes books with the best listings of temporary placement firms, executive, and legal recruiters. To order these books, e-mail **bookstore@kennedyinfo.com**.

## BOOKS

### The Directory of Temporary Placement Firms
For executives, managers, and professionals, it is categorized by industry, function, and geography.

### The Directory of Executive Recruiters
Published each year, this is the world's largest recruiter resource. Since these reference books are expensive, you may want to visit your public or college library. Use these directories to make sure that your résumé reaches the right person in the right firm.

## Chapter 10

# interviewing: a lifelong skill

# "getting to know you"

**Let your interview skills help break the ice**

Interviewing is not just a skill you'll use a couple of times in your life. You'll use it throughout your career—not only when trying to get a job, but also when getting to know your new coworkers or networking in your industry. How so? Think about it. A good interview is all about asking questions that reveal the most useful information. And asking questions is exactly what you'll need to do during your first weeks on the job. In a sense, you'll be the interviewer, and your job is to learn all you can about your new boss and coworkers. Your goal is twofold: to get your new coworkers to share valuable information about how to be successful on the job and to lay the foundation for good future working relationships.

Start with your coworkers. Now that you're part of the team, your new coworkers can give you the inside scoop on the organization. You'll want to ask them:

**What information is shared and how?** How information is handled tells you a lot about a company. In some companies, it is hoarded for power; in others it is shared, and if you don't share, you're not seen as a team player.

**How are decisions made?** Answers to this question will help flesh out how independent or dependent your boss is. Some bosses make decisions on their own; others require a great deal of input from everyone on their team. Are there certain people in the organization whose opinions seem to matter more than others?

**How is conflict handled?** What happens when things go wrong? Is blame immediately assigned to a person or the group? Is there an effort to learn from past mistakes?

**RED FLAG**

### Don't Pry

Always keep your questions focused on your job and the company. Make it clear that you are not interested in gossip or inside information.

# Getting to Know Your Boss

During these early days with your new boss, you'll be most anxious to make a good impression. That's only natural. But once you feel comfortable, see if you can't step back and get a bigger perspective on your job and your new boss. Try to see your boss as a human being, with both strengths and weaknesses. Use the interview skills that helped you read between the lines to help identify your boss's strengths and weaknesses. Here are some key characteristics to note.

**Skills:** What skills or knowledge areas does your boss lack? What does your boss hate to do? These represent great opportunities for you to focus on.

**Motivation:** What is your boss trying to accomplish in the organization? What gets her excited? What are the challenges facing her department, and how can you help meet them?

**Blind spots:** Where are the holes in your boss's networks? Where does communication break down?

**Communication style:** How does your boss prefer to receive information: just in time or with a long lead time; regularly or on a need-to-know basis? How much information does your boss want: complete details or the big picture? In what format, written or verbal?

**Decision-making style:** What decisions can you make unilaterally, and what decisions does your boss want to be involved in? Does your boss make decisions based on intuition or data? What does your boss need from you to make a decision (time, data, benchmarks, precedence)?

**Work style:** Does your boss prefer to work alone or with people? Is your boss a morning or night person? Is there an open-door policy? Does your boss thrive in chaos or prefer structure and order?

# exploratory interviews

## When you're ready to stretch your work horizon

You really like your job and you've been getting wonderful performance reviews. Great! But after a few years, you're starting to wonder what else is in store for you. In today's topsy-turvy employment world, you shouldn't rely on your boss to map out your next career move—*you* need to do that yourself. Enter the exploratory interview. This is where you poke around and talk with various people to learn about new job openings and/or projects. In fact, career counselors advise workers to conduct exploratory interviews with various people throughout the organization so that they will always be aware of important projects where they can really make an impact.

**Who should be the targets for your exploratory interviews?**
These are people who are "in the know." They are usually in managment spots and/or positions to make things happen.

**What to ask them?** Ask them what they're working on, challenges they're facing, or what they'd like to tackle. Find out what's in the pipeline: projects, jobs, or task forces that need to be staffed. These conversations can also help you identify a project that you can start up yourself.

**What to tell them?** Make it clear that you're looking for opportunities to have an impact in the company.

## FIRST PERSON SUCCESS STORY

### Strategic lunching

I had reached a dead end in my job and knew that if I wanted a promotion, I would have to prove myself somehow. I started having lunch with coworkers to find out what was going on. It turned out the market research team was not performing, so I set up an "informal" interview with the director to discuss what I could bring to the team. She was impressed by my enthusiasm and assigned me to the project. Our final report was widely praised and I was promoted to project manager—and got a big raise. Never underestimate the power of networking.

—Zachary H., Cedar Rapids, Iowa

# ASK THE EXPERTS

### I found out about a great job opening in another department. Should I tell my boss before I apply for it?

That's a tough one. You need to consider all the possible reactions your boss may have. Most bosses will be miffed at your desire to leave but won't stand in your way. Just know that once your boss knows that you're looking at other opportunities, your relationship will change. The power may shift in your favor: If he wants to keep you, he may try to make your present job more attractive. Or the power may shift against you: He may no longer see you as loyal, and any advancement in your current job will be all but nixed. If there's an unspoken rule in your company against departments "raiding" each other's employees, then your boss may be angry at your prospective boss for considering you.

### My boss's supervisor called me into her office to ask whether I was interested in being her new assistant. I'm not, but I don't want to offend her. What should I do?

This is a politically difficult situation, especially if your own boss knows nothing about this offer. No matter what you say, either your boss or your boss's supervisor is going to be unhappy. So, what can you do? If this new job doesn't take you in the direction you want your career to go, say so. Thank the supervisor, but explain how your current job is helping you gain the skills you need to achieve your next career step. If the problem is the personality of the supervisor, then thank her and describe how your current job is meeting your needs.

# networking interviews

## Keep your name out there

Even if you're perfectly happy in your new job, you should never stop looking toward your next one. This means keeping your résumé current, skimming the want ads and employment Web sites, and, most important of all, networking.

Networking, which is actually a type of interviewing, is all about staying in tune with the job marketplace, getting your name out there, and creating relationships with people who may someday help you find your next job.

You can network in endless ways: by joining professional associations, maintaining relationships with the major recruiters in your field, even having coffee with your HR manager. This allows you not only to keep an eye on the horizon, but to discover emerging trends in employment. Staying ahead of the trends and building your skills to be successful in emerging jobs and organizations is essential for your long-term career survival.

Networking also reveals the hidden job market. By most estimates, only 20 to 40 percent of job openings are advertised on the Web or in newspapers. Networking not only enables you to find out about those job openings, but increases the chances that people in your network will call you about an unlisted opening or give your name to someone else. With each new person you meet and add to your network, you have also added that person's whole list of contacts.

Finally, networking can build an attractive **Best Alternative to a Negotiated Agreement**. Through networking you may learn what your market value is or what kind of salary you could earn elsewhere so that when it's time for your salary review, you'll be better prepared to ask for what you're worth. If you continue to network and interview for other jobs, you may even end up with another job offer. Both situations give you a best alternative if your review with your current boss doesn't go as you'd like.

# The Coffee Project

**M**ake a list of people who work in your area of the company—superiors, peers, junior staff—and whom you don't know. Then, make a point of trying to have coffee with at least one person every week so that you can expand your network and increase your visibility. During this informal coffee break, you will be asking each person about his job and his work. Think of yourself as a reporter interviewing someone for a story.

"Hi, I'm from accounting and I was wondering if you'd like to get some coffee tomorrow morning to discuss (some subject that is work-related for both of you)." Agree on a time and place.

When you meet, thank your coworker for meeting with you. Talk about the work-related subject. Next, ask about any new projects that he's working on.

Here's an example of effective coffee networking:

"Thanks so much for meeting with me. I wanted to learn a little more about what you're doing so that I have a broader idea of what's happening in the company. I know you're working on the _____ project. Can you tell me about it?"

If your coworker doesn't say much, you can prompt him with: "How did you get assigned to that project? Who put the team together? Who's on the team with you? How are they to work with? What kinds of challenges are you facing? What have you enjoyed? What have you found difficult?"

End it by thanking your coworker for his time and saying how helpful the conversation has been in giving you a better understanding of the company.

# the exit interview

**Always end on a good note**

So you've landed your dream job. Great news. But now you have to say good-bye to your current employer. You will no doubt start by giving your boss notice of your departure. He may then contact human resources so that the process of termination can be started, including the nuts and bolts of transferring insurance and benefits.

Then, HR will most likely request an exit interview, which is standard practice in most companies. During the exit interview, departing employees discuss their job experiences and reasons for leaving. Like any other interview, you need to prepare for it.

**Be positive.** This is not the time to purge all the bitterness and unhappiness you've felt about the company. Even if you're leaving because of a miserable boss, low pay, or poor work/life balance, be careful how you share this information. Many career counselors would advise you to keep it to yourself, as sharing it will do you no good and may possibly come back to haunt you at a later date, say, when you need a job reference from your miserable boss.

**Be constructive.** Instead of complaining about how terribly you've been treated, talk proactively and strategically. Turn your complaints into positive suggestions for changes the company should make. This goes for changes you feel your boss should make, too.

**Be mindful.** Your goal is not to burn bridges, but to leave the company gracefully with solid relationships intact. You may never want to work there again, but you never know where those company employees may end up. That HR director conducting your exit interview today may be the HR director at another company you interview with 10 years from now!

## ASK THE EXPERTS

**The real reason I'm quitting is because my boss lied about some information in a report, and I don't want to work for a dishonest boss. Should I tell the HR person about this during my exit interview?**

If you have witnessed illegal activity, see a lawyer before you say anything in an exit interview. Mentioning it in an exit interview is equal to leveling a criminal charge, so make sure you're protected. If, instead, you've seen behavior that violates your ethics or morals, it's important for you to tell the HR person and get it on the record. Don't make a specific accusation (then you'd have to substantiate it). Instead, say something like, "My boss and I differ on what's ethical and moral. For that reason I need to leave the company."

**When and how do I tell my boss that I've been offered a job at a competitor's company?**

Your desire to take a new job should not come as a surprise to your current manager. Ideally, past conversations with him have revealed your career goals. However, you need to anticipate your boss's reaction. As soon as you think you may want to accept the competitor's offer, you need to talk to your current boss; don't wait until you hand in your two weeks' notice! After you tell your boss, he might try to redefine your present job to make you happy. If so, have a list of challenging projects you'd like to work on. If you think his reaction will be to block your efforts or at least make your life miserable, then wait until you have finalized the agreement with the new employer to tell him.

# now what do I do?

## Answers to common questions

### I've been offered a job at a competitor's company. When I told my boss, he offered to give me a bonus if I stay on. What should I do?

If you don't want to stay, thank your boss for the bonus offer, but explain that this new job offers different opportunities that you'd like to try. If you decide to take the bonus money and stay, then make sure you get the offer or any other sweeteners (extra vacation days, time off, etc.) in writing. If your boss refuses to give you a written offer, then take the new job.

### My boss is out ill and she's asked me to interview someone who would ultimately be working with me. I've never done this before. What should I do?

Don't fret. This is a great compliment—your boss is trusting you with a key management function. It could mean that you're in line for a promotion. Before the interview, take some time and prepare a few questions that will help you decide which candidate: 1) has the skills to do the job, 2) is motivated, and 3) would fit in with your group. (For more on interview techniques, see Chapter 3.) Here are some general guidelines.

■ Don't spend too much time chatting. Try to get down to business within five minutes.

■ Don't allow the applicant to be vague, evasive, or rambling. Interrupt them politely with, "Excuse me. Let me stop you there. What I wanted to know was . . ." If redirecting them doesn't work, ask questions that require a yes/no or very specific answer. You could say, "I'm confused. So are you saying you've had experience in this software language or not?"

■ Test for fit. Give the applicant scenarios of work situations she'd likely encounter in the job, then ask her how she'd handle it. If you know her proposed action would never work in your organization, prompt her to think differently about the situation. For example, "What if your boss would be angry if you took the problem to his boss, as you've suggested?" If the applicant still can't come up with an idea that would work, then she may have trouble fitting in with your organization's rules and culture.

■ Test the applicant's mettle. You don't want to bully a candidate, but you also may want to test her convictions or see how she'll act under the pressure your organization faces. One way to do this is to give a choice between two equally unsavory options. For example, "You've made your revenue target, but you could exceed it by laying off some support staff. What would you do?"

■ It's a two-way street. While you're considering the candidate, she is considering you. There's nothing more frustrating than finding the perfect candidate who doesn't want you. So treat applicants politely, don't keep them waiting, and give them plenty of opportunity to ask you questions.

# now where do I go?

## BOOKS

### Managing the Interview
by Susan Carol Curzon
Tips on interviewing others.

## WEB SITES

### Post your résumé and access job listings:

Job Finders Guide
**www.jobfindersonline.com**

Career Mosaic
**www.careermosaic.com**

JOBTRACK
**www.jobtrack.com**
Accessible to students/alumni of selected schools.

Yahoo! Classifieds
**http://classifieds.yahoo.com/employment.html**

## Network on message boards and in chat rooms, get job listings, post résumés, and get career planning advice:

Career Center for Workforce Diversity
**www.eop.com**
For minorities, women, and people with disabilities.

Career Paradise
**www.service.emory.edu/CAREER/Main/Links.html**

## Career links:

The Monster Board
**www.monster.com**

National Association of Colleges and Employers
**www.jobweb.org**

The Riley Guide
**www.rileyguide.com**

# glossary

**Age Discrimination in Employment Act** Passed in 1978, this federal law prohibits employers from discriminating against people age 40 or over. In some states, this age is as young as 18.

**Americans with Disabilities Act** Passed in 1990, this federal law prohibits discrimination based on mental or physical disabilities, as long as those disabilities do not prevent you from doing the job.

**Anchoring a negotiation** The first figure put on the table generally anchors, or sets the parameters for, a negotiation.

**Aptitude tests** These tests measure reasoning, mathematical, writing, or verbal skills. While the tests appear similar to skills tests, there is a significant difference: A skills test determines whether you can perform the job now, and the aptitude test determines whether you can be trained to do the job in the future.

**BATNA** or **Best Alternative to a Negotiated Agreement** Your best alternative if you do not reach an agreement in a current negotiation. States what you will do if you don't get what you want in the current negotiation.

**Behavioral interviews** Interviewers ask prepared questions about your past performance to ascertain how you are likely to respond in future situations. The prepared questions are based on the skills required for the job.

**Body language** The messages you convey through your facial expressions, eye contact, gestures, handshake, and posture.

**Business card** Many job seekers print up personal business cards to hand out when networking or interviewing. At the least, these cards include your name and contact information (address, phone, e-mail). Some cards include photographs and a brief compilation of skills and qualifications.

**Career coach** People qualified through their credentials and experience to use various psychological tools to help you figure out which jobs suit your interests, values, and talents.

**Case question interviews** These can range from one-sentence scenarios to one-page descriptions of a business problem. Interviewers are assessing how you think through problems and use data and your solutions to problems.

**Civil Rights Act** Passed in 1964, this federal law prohibits discrimination in employment based on race, sex, national origin, ancestry, or religious beliefs.

**Concessions** When one or both sides give up some of their demands to reach an agreement in a negotiation.

**Contingency fee executive search firms** Hiring organizations pay these firms only if they find and place a person in a job.

**Conversational interview questions** The interviewer asks a series of questions that are specific to a candidate and driven by the content of the applicant's résumé.

**Counteroffer** When one of two negotiating parties offers a change or concession from an original offer in an attempt to reach a zone of agreement.

**Culture of organization** A shorthand way of defining this term is "the way we do things around here." Like individuals, organizations have processes and behaviors that are deemed socially acceptable and others that are not. Arguing forcefully, for example, is a behavior that is accepted in some organizations, but not in others.

**Deal breaker** In a negotiation, this is a point that one side will not concede, or a requirement that is non-negotiable.

**Drug tests** Federal law requires that some companies, such as those in transportation, test prospective employees for drug use. Other companies use drug testing as a condition of hiring and continued employment. The most commonly used method of drug testing is urine sampling.

**Elevator speech** When you are job hunting, this is your 30-second declaration of the goal of your search and a one- or two-sentence statement of your qualifications for a job. The name derives from the idea of meeting someone in an elevator and having 30 seconds to tell him or her about what kind of work you are looking for.

**Employment agencies** These firms fill entry- and mid-level jobs and make their money by working in high volume with a number of employers. The hiring company usually pays the fees for an employment agency. Do not work with an employment agency that requires you to pay a fee.

**Employment lawyers** Attorneys who specialize in laws that pertain to hiring, working conditions, and firing.

**Executive recruiters** Placement specialists hired by companies to screen job candidates for high-level positions. Executive recruiters like to work with people who are presently employed.

**Exit interviews** Many companies conduct exit interviews with employees who are leaving the organization. Usually conducted by human resources, the interviews include questions about the employees' reasons for leaving and their general experiences working there. Companies use this information to identify ways to improve their ability to attract and retain good employees.

**Exploratory interviews** Similar to informational interviews, these interviews are conversations you have with people throughout your organization in order to identify projects, jobs, or other emerging work opportunities.

**Fallback position** As part of a negotiating strategy, one side or both have alternative solutions that avoid loss or failure.

**Fishing expeditions** When organizational leaders want to learn about the job seekers on the market, they will post a job opening that they may, or may not, fill.

**Fit** One of the most influential but often unconscious factors determining your attractiveness to interviewers. They want to know whether you'll be able to establish mutually respectful relationships and follow the often unwritten rules of behavior—and thereby successfully produce results for the organization.

**Gatekeepers** The people who guard an organization's door. They are often HR people who screen job candidates and pass qualified candidates on to hiring managers. Always be courteous to gatekeepers!

**Gender expectations** Every culture has "rules" dictating appropriate behavior for men and women. These rules may be unspoken but are nevertheless passed down the generations through the media, literature, platitudes, folklore, religion, etc. Men are expected to behave one way, women another. When interacting, each gender expects the other to follow those rules.

**Hidden job market** Jobs that executives can and may fill by searching for candidates through informal mechanisms, such as networking.

**Hiring manager** The person who has the authority to hire you—or not. Often, this is also the person you report to directly once on the job.

**Honesty tests** These tests have evolved from employers' concerns about employee theft. These tests are administered when employees handle money, merchandise, or customer accounts.

**Hypothetical interview questions** The interviewer asks you to imagine a situation and then explain how you would respond to the described events.

**Illegal interview questions** Some questions that are not related to the job are forbidden by law, such as questions regarding age, sex, race, national origin, citizenship, religion, physical ability, and family life.

**Immigration Reform and Control Act** Passed in 1986, this prohibits discrimination against legal aliens based on national origin or citizenship status.

**Informational interviews** The surface reason for an informational interview is for you to talk with a knowledgeable expert about careers or industries that interest you. The unspoken reason is for you to determine whether the expert knows about jobs for which you might be qualified or whether she can pass on your name and résumé to people who hire.

**Influencer** A person who does not have hiring authority, but who can be influential in supporting or derailing your candidacy. Be nice to influencers.

**Interview** In this book, an interview is defined as a purposeful conversation between you and an HR manager, screener, or recruiter to determine if an organization wants to hire you; or a conversation with a colleague, job fair representative, or job coach about job openings, the job market, your job search, or anything else related to employment.

**Job fairs** Gatherings of lots of employers in one place, such as a convention hall or the ballroom of a major hotel. The goal of the employers is to meet large numbers of job seekers quickly and to collect lots of résumés that can be screened for qualified candidates. When the economy is strong, there are many job or career fairs to attend.

**Job language** The jargon used by people in a particular job or industry. It is wise to use the language of the job for which you are applying.

**"Leave money on the table"** An expression used in negotiations to describe when a prospective employee does not ask for as much money as an employer was willing to pay.

**Likeability** This stems from how warm, positive, empathetic, and interesting you are. While an interviewer will try to minimize the effect liking you has on his hiring decision, with all other things equal, he'll hire the person with whom he'll enjoy working.

**Negotiating range** The low to high range of expectations for salary in a negotiation.

**Network** Your network is made up of personal and professional relationships with people who know what you do, want to do, and can do. These people are invaluable sources of information and can connect you to people who are hiring. You are also part of their networks and, as such, should provide them information and connections to others.

**Nonprofit organizations** Under federal and state incorporation and tax laws, founders must declare the purpose and mission of their organizations and classify them. Leaders of nonprofit organizations must channel excessive resources back into the organization rather than distribute it to individuals.

**Opening position** The first offer in a negotiation.

**Other side** In negotiating, remember to refer to the person who sits on the opposite side of the table as "the

other side." This language may reduce the heat that can occur in a tough negotiation.

**Outsourcing** This growing trend in organizations, in which temporary workers are contracted to perform specific tasks, can serve as a threat (can your job be outsourced?) or an opportunity (can you be a contract worker?) to job seekers.

**Packaging** Rather than just advocating for your interests and needs in a negotiation, you discover the interests and needs of the other side and put together a package that meets the interests of both sides.

**Panel interview** Instead of interviewing you one-on-one, a company will gather a group of staff to interview you.

**Personality tests** These tests provide employers with a profile of you along certain dimensions, such as adaptability, flexibility, creativity, and/or control of temper. Employers may test you only for traits that are relevant to the performance of the job.

**Personal language** This is your own individual style of speaking, such as fast or slow, direct or indirect. It's important to try to identify your interviewer's personal language and speak that way.

**Positioning statement** This brief introduction of yourself is useful while networking or answering an interviewer's "tell me about yourself" question. In two minutes or less, include a brief summary of your education and work experience, three to four of your main strengths, and your career aspirations.

**Pregnancy Discrimination Act** Passed in 1978, this federal law prohibits discrimination in hiring or during employment of pregnant women or women with pregnancy-related medical conditions.

**Presentation interview** To gauge your public speaking or stress management skills, you may be asked to make a presentation to an audience as part of the interview process.

**Protected class** A group of people protected by state or federal law against discrimination. You cannot be discriminated against on the basis of age, race, sex, national origin, ancestry, religion, or physical or mental disabilities.

**Quantifying** An interview technique that involves numerically measuring the scope of an outcome you produced. To make a more powerful impression when you are talking about something you produced, quantify it ("saved three days" instead of "saved time").

**References** People (prior bosses, business associates, friends, community leaders) you've chosen for prospective employers to talk to about you and your qualifications.

**Résumé** A one- to two-page document that describes your educational and professional experiences. It can also include lists of publications, awards, professional association memberships, and specific skills.

**Retained executive recruiting firms** Hiring companies place these firms on a year or longer contract and pay them regularly scheduled fees to search for qualified candidates.

**Salary range** The low to high range of money you can request for a job.

**Screeners** People, often in a company's human resources department, who preview résumés and job seekers and forward qualified candidates to hiring managers.

**Sexual dynamics** A normal dynamic of attraction that can occur between interviewer and interviewee. A wise interviewee doesn't act on it.

**Sexual harassment** State and federal laws define this as unwanted sexual advances or visual, verbal, or physical conduct of a sexual nature that interferes with your ability to work.

**Skills test** The employer asks an applicant to demonstrate the skills needed for the job. For example, a pilot would be expected to show that she can fly a plane.

**Strategic interviewing** A strategic job applicant asks the interviewer questions to ascertain what the company's current concerns are, and then positions herself as helping resolve those concerns.

**Stress interview** The purpose of a stress interview is to test how you respond under very difficult circumstances. Interviewers can create stressful situations by using harsh, judgmental questions, by interrupting you as you attempt to respond to questions, or by having several interviewers in the room at once.

**Stretch assignment** A component of a job that is not presently part of your skill set. Accomplishing the task will require you to grow beyond your present capabilities.

**Success stories** Two-minute stories about past accomplishments by you used throughout the interview process to illustrate your skills and competencies. Each story should include a concise description of a problem, challenge, or opportunity you faced in the past, what you did about it, and what the positive outcome was.

**Surface differences** When interviewing, you want to get beyond any visible surface diversity, such as your race or age, and make deeper connections with your interviewer based on values, beliefs, or priorities.

**Temporary placement firms** Companies hire these agencies to search for, screen, and often hire candidates for temporary positions. Since the early 1990s, more and more temporary placement firms are placing white-collar workers.

**Transferable skills** Skills you've developed in past jobs that you carry with you into the next job. Skills in project management, public speaking, grant writing, conflict resolution, or team leadership are examples.

**White-collar staff** The term "white collar" comes from the turn of the nineteenth century, when people working in offices could keep their collars clean throughout a day's labor in contrast to factory workers. Today the term generally refers to people who work in offices.

**Win-win negotiating strategy** An approach in which both parties in a negotiation can get their needs met through effective communication and problem-solving techniques.

**Working interview** Infrequently an organization will ask you to come and "work" for a specified time period. You need to negotiate whether you'll be paid for your time.

**Work/life balance** A growing concern of the labor force as more employees seek ways to have time for both professional and personal growth.

# index

# P

# Q

# R

## S

salary, 152-153
    being ready to discuss, 14
    in career change, 94
    negotiating range, 157
    nonnegotiable *versus* negotiable, 153
    of previous job, 153
    requirements asked early on, 57
    researching the marketplace, 152
    Web sites, 165
same-sex partner, 120
screeners, 14-15
    interviewing with, 175
second interview, 46-47, 122-147
setting the right tone, 54-55
sex discrimination, 119
sexual harassment, 115
signing documents, 160
skills. *See also* transferable skills
    showcasing to future boss, 125
skill sets, 53
skill tests, 36
spouse's transfer, 99
standardized personality tests, 184
state unemployment insurance and job hunters
        group, 173
step down, taking a, 100-101
stereotypes
    cultural, 117
    older workers, 108-109
    younger workers, 110
strategic interviewing, 126-127
stress interview, 78-79
styles of interviews, 70-85
success stories
    in behavior-based interviews, 80
    for career change interview, 94
    crafting, 16
    disabilities and, 112
    examples, 17
    quantifying results, 18, 19
    showing how they benefited the organization, 19
    START format, 16
    told to future boss, 125
support
    from job seekers groups, 172
    for retired military personnel, 102

## T

temporary placement firms, 174, 178-179
    directory of, 185
tests, 36
    preparing for, 37
    standardized personality tests, 184
    temporary placement firms and, 179
thank-you letters, 14
    after interview, 66
    to members of a panel, 129
    to references, 28
    sample, 67
third round of interviews, 46-47
time off, explaining, 98-99
title of new job, 164-165
transferable skills
    for career change, 91, 92, 94
    success stories illustrating, 17
traps in conversational interview, 74
travel expenses, 139
typing tests, 36

## U

underqualification, 168, 169

## V

vacation time, negotiating for more, 164
*Vault Guide to the Case Interview, The*, 83
videoconferencing, 140-141
volunteering at a nonprofit organization
        and career change, 92
        and reentry in the workplace, 185

## W

weaknesses, identifying your, 13
Web sites
    business etiquette, 41
    career counselor, 171
    case interviews, 85
    company information, 103, 154, 165
    employees with disabilities, 113, 121
    entry-level jobs, 41
    http://career.boisestate.edu/etiquette.html, 41
    http://cba.uiuc.edu/general/jobs/search/
        etiq.html, 41
    http://classifieds.yahoo.com/employment.html,
        197

# about the authors

**Cynthia Ingols** and **Mary Shapiro** are professors at Simmons School of Management in Boston where they team-teach a course entitled Career Strategies in the MBA program, which focuses on the art of interviewing. In addition to teaching, Cynthia Ingols consults with Fortune 500 companies, developing interactive executive education programs, coaching managers to enhance their careers, and conducting organizational diagnostic work to promote innovation and creativity. She has written award-winning case studies used in several MBA programs. Mary Shapiro has been a consultant, executive trainer, and a Simmons MBA faculty member for over 20 years. During that time she has specialized in the fields of team leadership, persuasive communication, and career strategies. She has worked with companies ranging from Merck Pharmaceuticals to Harvard University.

The authors would like to thank **Kristin Heath**, **Denise Davis**, **Dean Patricia O'Brien**, **Cheryl McLean**, **Pat Mallion**, **Deb Kadaner**, and other Simmons School of Management alumni, faculty, and staff for their help in writing this book.

Silver Lining Books would like to thank the following consultants for their help in preparing this book: **Ruth K. Robbins** of Career Momentum/Résumés Plus in New York City, and a certified counselor of the Five O' Clock Club; and **Colleen Stewart**, an executive recruiter in Atlanta, Georgia.

**Barbara J. Morgan** Publisher, Silver Lining Books

**Barnes & Noble Basics**
**Barb Chintz** Editorial Director
**Leonard Vigliarolo** Design Director

**Barnes & Noble Basics**™ *Your Job Interview*
**Wynn Madrigal** Editor
**Elizabeth McNulty** Editorial Production Coordinator
**Leslie Stem** Design Assistant
**Emily Seese** Editorial Assistant
**Della R. Mancuso** Production Manager